WHAT REALLY MATTERS FOR STRUGGLING READERS

Designing Research-Based Programs

WHAT REALLY MATTERS FOR STRUGGLING READERS

Designing Research-Based Programs

Richard L. Allington
University of Florida

New York San Francisco Boston
London Toronto Sydney Tokyo Singapore Madrid
Mexico City Munich Paris Cape Town Hong Kong Montreal

Acquisitions Editor: Aurora Martinez
Marketing Manager: Kathleen Morgan
Production Manager: Ellen MacElree
Project Coordination, Text Design, and Electronic Page Makeup: Electronic Publishing Services Inc., N.Y.C.
Cover Design Manager: Wendy Ann Fredericks
Cover Designer: Wendy Stolberg
Senior Manufacturing Buyer: Dennis J. Para
Printer and Binder: The Maple Vail Book Manufacturing Group
Cover Printer: Phoenix Color Corps

Library of Congress Cataloging-in-Publication Data
Allington, Richard L.
    What really matters for struggling readers : designing research-based programs /
Richard L. Allington.
       p. cm.
    Includes bibliographical references (p.) and index.
    ISBN 0-321-06396-1 (pbk.)
    1. Reading--Remedial teaching--United States. 2. Reading--Research--United
States--methodology. I. Title.
    LB1050.5 .A452001
    372.43--dc21   00-042841

Please visit our website at http://www.awl.com

ISBN 0-321-06396-1

10 11 12 13--MA--06 05 04

CONTENTS

PREFACE

I intend this book to be a useful response to recent legislation emphasizing the selection of instructional interventions based on "reliable, replicable scientific research." I am writing this text because of the many narrow interpretations of what the research says (as well as the published blatant distortions of what the research says). We have learned much about the design and delivery of more effective literacy instruction in the past thirty years and much of what we have learned is being systematically ignored in the current wave of high-stakes reform. I intend this book to be practical. I hope that the design of the chapters provide sufficient guidance to allow readers to create more effective interventions for struggling readers. These might be classroom instructional improvement initiatives, summer school or after-school interventions, or simply the redesign of remedial and special education services.

Each chapter includes a brief review of the key research literature in order to point to the "scientific" nature of my proposals. An annotated bibliography of the most important studies I cite is available on the publisher's website (www.awl.com) and readers can turn there to find details of the research I have purposely omitted here in the interest of interestingness.

You will note that there is no chapter on phonemic awareness and none on phonics. This was not an oversight. Nor was it intended to suggest that I think either of these topics is unimportant, especially for struggling readers. Both are important and both are covered extensively in the first book published in this series of Cunningham and Allington books. That book is Pat Cunningham's *Phonics They Use* (Longman, 2000), now in its third edition. In addition, the longest chapter in our coauthored book, *Classrooms That Work* (Longman, 1999) is focused on phonemic awareness and phonics. And there has been a flurry of other recent books on these topics. But there are few books on the topics I have elected to write about in this book—topics such as the importance of reading volume, access to books, especially books of appropriate difficulty and interest, on developing reading fluency, and fostering thoughtful literacy through promoting literate conversations. It's not that no books exist on these topics but that none seem to pull all these topics together, yet it is these things that I believe really matter for struggling readers.

Richard L. Allington

ACKNOWLEDGMENTS

Dr. Gay Ivey, *University of Maryland*
Dr. Evangeline Newton, *University of Akron*
Dr. Charity St. Clair, *San Diego Unified School District*
Dr. Hope Elkins, *Indiana University*
Dr. Patrick P. McCabe, *Nova Southeastern University*

READING INSTRUCTION IN AMERICAN SCHOOLS

For two decades American education has suffered a steady barrage of criticism from politicians, policy makers, and pundits. As a result, many have accepted what Berliner and Biddle (1995) called "the manufactured crisis" as based in fact. Questions about American children's reading proficiency has been a central theme in the negative education campaigning. Today, many adults believe that American schoolchildren have fallen behind children in other nations and that illiteracy is rampant across the nation. Teachers are seen as largely ill-trained, with one federal official offering his opinion that fewer than 10 percent of American elementary teachers are adequately prepared to teach children how to read.

Not surprisingly, on the heels of the negative portrayals have come a veritable flood of suggestions for how to best reform American schooling and set schools (and teachers) back on the "right" course. There seems no end to the supply of ideas about how to change the American educational system. The national standards movement with high-stakes testing has been promoted as one vehicle for improving schooling. So too has the proposals for "school choice" and the accompanying vouchers that are seen as a way to put an entrepreneurial spirit into the educational industry. Alternative teacher certification plans and, perhaps, eliminating college-based teacher education have also been suggested. And, of course, there is the call for a "return to phonics" in the teaching of beginning reading as a specific solution for the lagging performance of American children as readers.

There is a new enthusiasm for "research-based" decisions in education, especially in the design of early reading programs. The Federal Reading Excellence Act and a number of state education laws now demand "rigorous, replicable, scientific evidence" to support the design of reading instruction and the selection of reading materials.

So, here I sit at my computer writing yet another book on improving reading instruction. Why another book and why now?

National Reading Panel

(*www.nationalreadingpanel.org*)

The National Reading Panel (NRP) was charged by Congress with recommending the scientific studies that were worthy of consideration in the design of reading instruction in the future. The NRP elected to examine only the experimental research studies in developing their report, a decision decried by many educational researchers. Based on their review of this body of research they concluded:

- developing phonemic awareness and phonics skills in Kindergarten and first grade was supported by the research
- providing regular guided oral reading with a focus on fluency was important
- silent reading was recommended for developing fluency, vocabulary and comprehension skills (though the Panel felt that the research reviewed had not adequately demonstrated the benefits of sustained silent reading practice)
- direct teaching of comprehension strategies was recommended and it was noted that providing good comprehension strategy instruction is a complex instructional activity. Thus, the Panel recommend extensive, formal preparation in comprehension strategies teaching for all teachers
- Finally, the NRP notes that little research is available to support the use of technology (e.g., computers) in teaching reading but the few studies available suggest that it is possible that there is a potential for some benefits to students

Why Another Book?

Because it seems to me that much of the rhetoric and policy making that surrounds current efforts at "reforming" American reading instruction is misguided. Misguided because much of the reform sentiment focuses on features of instruction that don't really matter that much in the grand scheme of things. Many of the reforms are narrowly conceived and simply cannot have the sort of impact that we might hope for given the time, money, and energy that will be spent. In this book I hope to refocus the reader's attention on the few things that really matter in teaching children to read (and the things over which we as teachers and administrators can actually exert a degree of control).

Why Now?

Simply, the reason for writing another book now is that we are about to begin to feel the impact of the Reading Excellence Act on the design of school reading programs. I am writing because I am worried that, to date, "What the research says…" has been narrowly interpreted and focused almost wholly on the very beginning stages of reading instruction. I am writing because I am deeply worried that so much of what we have learned about teaching reading effectively—especially to children who have difficulty—is being routinely ignored. I am writing because the research is being misrepresented (See Allington & Woodside-Jiron, 1998; 1999; Allington, 1999; Taylor, 1998; Coles, 2000.) I am writing because much of what might prove useful instructionally in first grade is being misapplied to older children and to children having difficulty.

My goal is to provide a readable, practical treatise on designing a more effective reading instruction. My long-standing concern for children who find learning to read difficult will be evident because it is the instruction of those children that seems most often to go awry in schools.

But to begin, let me try and correct some of the misunderstandings about American children's reading proficiency and American reading instruction as we enter the new millennium.

So How Bad is the Situation in Terms of Reading Achievement?

Actually, the answer depends on your reference point. For instance, in the most recent international comparisons of children's reading achievement (Elley, 1992), American fourth graders were ranked second in the world, behind only the Finnish children (See Table 1.1.) American ninth graders ranked right in the middle, at the international average (See Table 1.2.) These data often surprise many Americans, including educators. But as they say, "You can look it up!" In addition, there are aspects to these data that deserve more exposure. The most economically disadvantaged American students "performed at about the

TABLE 1.1
Countries Ranked by Fourth–Grade Reading Achievement: Total Score

Country	Mean	Standard Error	Country	Mean	Standard Error
Finland	569	3.4			
United States	547	2.8			
Sweden	539	2.8	Germany (West)	503	3.0
France	531	4.0	Canada (British Columbia)	500	3.0
Italy	529	4.3	Germany (East)	499	4.3
New Zealand	528	3.3	Hungary	499	3.1
Norway	524	2.6	Slovenia	498	2.6
Iceland*	518	0.0	Netherlands	485	3.6
Hong Kong	517	3.9	Cyprus	481	2.3
Singapore	515	1.0	Portugal	478	3.6
Switzerland	511	2.7	Denmark	475	3.5
Ireland	509	3.6	Trinidad/Tobago	451	3.4
Belgium (French)	507	3.2	Indonesia	394	3.0
Greece	504	3.7	Venezuela	383	3.4
Spain	504	2.5			

*Iceland tested all students, therefore no standard error was calculated.

■ Mean achievement higher than United States

■ Mean achievement equal to United States

■ Mean achievement lower than United States

Source: Elley, Warwick B., *How in the World Do Students Read?*, The Hague: International Association for the Evaluation of Educational Achievement, 1992.

TABLE 1.2
Countries Ranked by Ninth–Grade Reading Achievement: Total Score

Country	Mean	Standard Error	Country	Mean	Standard Error
Finland	560	2.5			
France	549	4.3	Singapore	534	1.1
Sweden	546	2.5	Slovenia	532	2.3
New Zealand	545	5.6	Germany (East)	526	3.5
Hungary	536	3.3	Denmark	525	2.1
Iceland	536	0.0	Portugal	523	3.1
Switzerland	536	3.2	Canada (British Columbia)	522	3.0
Hong Kong	535	3.7	Germany (West)	522	4.4
United States	535	4.8	Netherlands	514	4.9
Norway	516	2.3	Trinidad/Tobago	479	1.7
Italy	515	3.4	Thailand*	477	6.2
Ireland	511	5.2	Philippines	430	3.9
Greece	509	2.9	Venezuela	417	3.1
Cyprus	497	2.2	Nigeria*	401	___†
Spain	490	2.5	Zimbabwe*	372	3.8
Belgium (French)	481	4.9	Botswana	330	2.0

*Sampling response rate of schools below 80%.

†Insufficient data to calculate standard error.

■ Mean achievement higher than United States

■ Mean achievement equal to United States

■ Mean achievement lower than United States

Source: Elley, Warwick B., *How in the World Do Students Read?*, The Hague: International Association for the Evaluation of Educational Achievement, 1992.

international average in both grades" (Binkley & Williams, 1996, p. ix). So, if American elementary schools are failing, virtually all schools across the globe must be failing also. In other words, when compared to children in other nations, American elementary school children read as well or better than children of the same ages around the world. Virtually the same achievement patterns occur in science and mathematics, but that is another book.

If we look at the thirty-year history of the National Assessment of Educational Progress (NAEP)—the NAEP provides comparative historical data on the reading proficiency of fourth-, eighth-, and twelfth-graders—we find that in the 1999 NAEP, students recorded stable or rising reading achievement levels. U.S. Secretary of Education Riley has noted that fourth-grade scores have risen from one-third to one-half of a grade level in less than ten years. On the NAEP, fourth- and eighth-grade students' scores rose between 1970 and 1980, then declined modestly between 1980 and 1990 but have been rising across the 1990s. The performances of twelfth-grade students had been rising until 1990 and then declined modestly until the 1999 assessment where they again rose to previous achievement levels.

The achievement of American elementary and middle school students on nationally normed, standardized commercial tests of reading achievement have

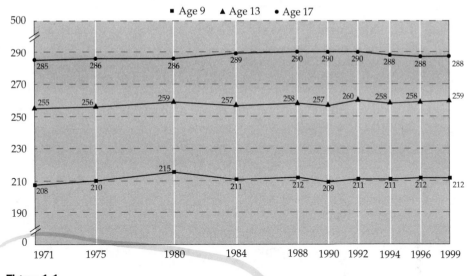

Figure 1.1
NAEP Reading Average Scale Scores for the Nation
Source: National Center for Education Statistics. National Assessment of Educational Progress
http://nces.ed.gov.

been rising since 1980. Between 1965 and 1980, the heyday of the skills instruction movement, these scores declined but began to rise substantially in recent years (Bracey, 1997). For instance, on the Iowa Test of Basic Skills, the average fifth-grader's achievement in 1990 roughly equaled the average sixth-grader's achievement in 1975, and the average third-grader's achievement in 1990 equaled the achievement of the average fourth-grader in 1955. Across the forty-five-year period (1955–1990), elementary school student achievement rose quite dramatically while average middle school achievement improved only modestly. But at all grade levels children today outperform children from earlier eras of American schooling

Finally, one other indicator that might be used are the readability formulas that were created to estimate the difficulty of books. The oldest and most popular of these formulas originated in the 1940s and 1950s. However, two such stalwarts—the Dale-Chall and the Spache readability formulas—were renormed in the 1980s because they no longer accurately reflected the grade difficulty of texts. In both cases, the difficulty estimates were overestimating the complexity. So in renorming, what had been a seventh-grade-level book became a sixth-grade-level book.

Various explanations for the wave of negative information that has filled the media have been offered but a simple principle for educational reporting— Good news is no news—may provide the simplest explanation. Of course, when advocates of privatization of education attempt to move their political agenda, bad news about American schools is necessary as a lever to attempt to persuade

Two plain language books that discuss American educational achievement patterns in detail are Gerald Bracey's, *Setting the Record Straight* (Association for Supervision and Curriculum Development, 1–800–933–2723.) and Richard Rothstein's, *The Way We Were?* (The Century Foundation, 1–800–552–5450). Both books cover broad academic achievement patterns for K–12 and include data on various other schooling issues such as flunking, teacher accountability, minority achievement, and so on.

the public to accept such a radical shift in the financing of public education (Bracey, 1997). And for two decades, through the 1980s and the 1990s, the White House was occupied by privatization advocates. But, interestingly, the American public seems more confused than convinced that American education is failing.

In a recent Gallup Poll (Coles, 1999), half of American adults awarded their local schools an A or B grade for effectiveness. However, fewer than half of these same adults awarded American schools generally the same grade. In other words, lots of folks believe their children attend one of the few good schools in the country. These adults award grades to local schools based on more direct knowledge of the achievements of those schools. They award lower grades when asked to rate schools that they have little direct knowledge of. These are schools that they acquire information about only indirectly, largely through media accounts. So it seems that most American adults believe that *other* schools need to improve but *their* schools are doing a very creditable job of educating children.

But if Achievement is Actually Rising, Why Another Book?

The research points to high reading achievement levels in American students as we begin a new century. No doubt about it. But the research also points to several disturbing trends in American reading achievement. The first is the trend for certain groups of children to lag behind their peers in literacy learning. And the more disturbing part is that these children are all too often predictable. For instance, researchers at the Rand Institute on Education and Training (Grissmer et al., 1994) found that students whose parents were not high school graduates had achievement levels significantly below the achievement levels of children whose parents were college graduates. Family income was also related to achievement. So was mother's age (with the children of older mothers achieving higher levels) and other factors. But, perhaps surprisingly, these researchers found little relationship between achievement and children from single-parent homes or homes where both parents worked. They concluded that only parent educational levels and family income were related to achievement.

Their analyses also showed that minority students earned lower average achievement than majority students. And although the gap between minority-majority achievement has narrowed over the past thiry years, the achievement differences are still substantial by the end of middle school. But because minority families are more often poor, when compared to majority families, some of the achievement differences are explained by the negative effects of more widespread poverty in minority communities.

Three Challenges.   Nonetheless, it would seem that American schools currently work better for children from certain sorts of families. In order to hope to fulfill the promise of public education, schools must work for all children—regardless of which parents the children got. So this is the first challenge of American education. Designing schools that are less parent-dependent. Designing schools where all children can expect to be successful readers and writers.

There is a second challenge for American education. That is that while we have been largely successful in teaching children to read and write at basic levels of proficiency, the "information age" places higher-order literacy demands on all of us. As Bill Kovack and Tom Rosenstiel point out in their hard-hitting book, *Warp Speed: America in the Age of Mixed Media* (Century Foundation, 1999), we have entered an age of unfettered information flow. Historically, only a few large publishers could afford to provide national news and information dissemination. They argue that with that power came a sense of responsibility for attempting to ensure an accuracy and completeness of the information. Journalistic codes of ethics, in other words. Editorial decisions about the quality of the "evidence" supporting a story and so on. They note that the modern information environment is very different with a proliferation of news outlets, twenty-four-hour news and infotainment channels. They point to a new "journalism of assertion" as the dominant mode of delivery. A mode that has fewer checks and balances and literally places far greater demands on the reader, viewer, listener. These demands include synthesizing and evaluating information from multiple sources. These multiple information sources have fewer editorial controls and fewer filters through which information is sifted for accuracy, reliability, and civility. And Kovack and Rosenstiel hardly even mention the Internet but instead focus on the television and print media.

The Internet imposes virtually no controls on information quality and reliability. Type the word *Holocaust* into an Internet search engine and you will find more web pages exist denying the Holocaust ever took place than pages offering reliable historical data. While materials denying the Holocaust have been around since the 1950s, never have they been so widely accessible to so many people. Never have they appeared so "official."

Because of the increase in the unfettered flow of information, American schools need to enhance the ability of children to search and sort through information, to synthesize and analyze information, and to summarize and evaluate the information they encounter. On the one hand, the performances of American students have been improving on the NAEP, having risen to historically high levels of attainment. On the other hand, only a few American students seem to be able to demonstrate even minimal proficiency with higher-order literacy strategies (and the children most likely to demonstrate these are those children whose parents have high levels of educational attainment). Even a quick examination of the NAEP items that so many children and adolescents find so difficult suggests that we have done a better job of teaching the basic literacy skills (word recognition, literal comprehension) than the higher-order, or -thinking, skills and strategies. The items attempting to assess higher-order proficiencies do not require rocket-scientist type performances. Many, in fact, require little more than the sorts of judgments about information, ideas, and assertions that an adult might need to make nearly every day.

There is a third challenge for American education that needs to be mentioned. Our schools create more students who *can* read than students who *do* read. Too many students and adults read only when they are required to. Interest in voluntary reading begins to fall in the upper-elementary grades and declines steeply in middle school and continues to fall across high school. We seem to be producing readers who can read more difficult texts but readers who elect not to read even easy texts on their own time.

American schools, especially American elementary schools, produce children who rank among the world's best readers. The schools are improving. More children are better readers than ever before. But there are still substantial challenges that need to be confronted.

Sample Items from a Recent Fourth Grade NAEP.

After the students read a two and one-half page Ashanti folktale entitled, "Hungry Spider and the Turtle," the following written response questions were posed:

- There is a saying, "Don't get mad, get even." How does this apply to the story?
- Who do you think would make a better friend, Spider or Turtle? Explain why.
- Think about Spider and Turtle in the story. Pick someone you know, have read about, or have seen in the movies or on television and explain how that person is like either Spider of Turtle.

In each of these short written responses students had to *think* about the story, not just recall the story (though recalling characters and their traits noted in the story is obviously essential to responding adequately). The point to be made is that being able to locate or remember the correct answer (word or phrase) to a multiple-choice item, the traditional measure of comprehension, is simply much less demanding than responding to these new measures of reading comprehension.

Can Educational Research Provide Support for Meeting these Challenges?

Perhaps. We have learned much about what sorts of schools, classrooms, and lessons foster reading proficiency. We have learned about how to redesign schools and classrooms and lessons to better meet the needs of children who find learning difficult. We have also been learning more about what sorts of classrooms and lessons foster the higher-order literacy that seems often neglected. And we have learned more than a little about the sorts of classrooms and lessons that foster ownership of reading and writing. But with all we have learned, there still exists no simple blueprint for restructuring schools, classrooms, and lessons. Perhaps that is because blueprints differ for virtually every building constructed. Perhaps the same is true of school restructuring. Because we build different buildings for different clients, we may need to build different classrooms and lessons for different students in order to meet the challenges that confront us.

In suggesting that educational research can provide no blueprint I am not suggesting that educational research can provide no guidelines—quite the contrary. But educational research is a slippery beast. There is a trove of published studies and an even greater supply of unpublished studies to be found in ERIC and Dissertation Abstracts. Much of the educational research available, even in the published papers, fails to meet rigorous quality criteria. Skeptics suggest that, "You can prove anything with research." To some extent that is true, especially at the level of comparing particular programs, materials, or methods. Such comparisons have a long history in education even though the results are rarely consistent from study to study. Too often, proponents of a particular method, material, or program selectively review the available research and report on studies supporting their biases. A more comprehensive review often shifts the resulting conclusions.

It is not uncommon to hear someone initiate a discussion of any particular method, material, or program with the phrase, "Hundreds of studies show…" Truth be told, it is impossible to locate 100 studies showing the same effect for any method, material, or program. Consider that Jeanne Chall, author of *Learning to Read: The Great Debate* (1983) located fewer than 100 studies comparing different approaches to teaching beginning reading even though her review covered the first eighty years of this century. Every approach she examined produced the best results in at least one of the comparison studies and every approach was found less effective in some studies. Similar findings after twenty seven coordinated studies compared methods and materials in the largest beginning reading field experiment ever conducted, led the authors of the *First Grade Studies* (Bond & Dykstra, 1967) to conclude: "Children learn to read by a variety of materials and methods…. No one approach is so distinctly better in all situations and respects than the others that it should be considered the one best method…" (p. 75).

On most educational questions there are only a handful of published studies and often these are smallish and local. In the case of materials and programs the number of published studies shrinks even further. Additionally, more often than not, the majority of the few published studies are authored by the developers and marketers of the materials and programs. In other words, there are few independent evaluations of most materials and programs available. Several examples come to mind.

First, there is the Higher Order Thinking Skills (HOTS) program. This upper-grade program utilizes computer-aided lessons to foster reading development and, particularly, reading comprehension. While widely implemented, virtually all of the published papers on the effects of the HOTS program have been authored (or coauthored) by the developer (e.g., Pogrow, 1990, 1993). Then there is the Accelerated Reader program, again, widely implemented but almost no published research is available and no experimental independent studies have been published in the research journals. In both these cases, newsletters or privately produced "in-house" magazines routinely offer testimonials, case studies, and reports of achievement effects. But publishing a positive puff-piece in an "in-house" magazine or newsletter does not offer the same sort of evidence of effects as would independent studies published in recognized, peer-reviewed research journals.

Then there is the heavily promoted Success for All (SFA) program and the highly publicized Direct Instruction (DI) materials. In both these cases there exists a substantial set of studies, often published in professional journals (with fewer studies published in peer-reviewed research journals). In both cases there are some independent research studies that have also been published. The sets of SFA studies generally find that the program produces statistically significant achievement effects when SFA schools are compared to control schools (schools without SFA). The independent studies report the same sort of effects, though often reporting smaller differences in achievement between schools than the studies by the SFA developers. There exists, then, published evidence that implementing the SFA program improves achievement.

However, as Venezky (1998) points out in his reanalysis of the SFA data, the program continues to produce large numbers of children with dismayingly low reading achievement. He reported that fifth-grade students in the SFA schools had reading achievement levels at the middle-third-grade level compared to the beginning-third-grade reading levels of fifth graders in the control schools. Venezky does not question whether SFA produced higher achievement levels—it did. Rather, he asks whether we are willing to accept *so little* improvement in reading as sufficient evidence that the SFA program should be recommended for wide implementation.

In the case of the DI materials, the body of research extends back thirty years and the evidence has been controversial across that period of time (e.g., House, et al. 1978; Schweinhart & Weikart, 1998). The majority of the DI research has been done by the developers with much of it reported in *Effective School Practices*, the in-house magazine of the Association for Direct Instruction edited by one of the DI program authors. More recently, this research was summarized in a selective review (Adams & Englemann, 1996)—a review that omitted a number of DI studies that did not report positive effects. There are so few independent studies published in peer-reviewed research journals that some scholars largely discount the evidence available (Stahl et al., 1998).

This sort of criticism could just as easily be offered on Reading Recovery, whole language, Alphabetic Phonics, and the Houghton-Mifflin (or any other major publisher) reading program. The important point here is that "What the research says..." is currently an almost meaningless phrase. In other words, virtually every proponent of any method, material, or program can find some sort of evidence what they have to offer that works somewhere, some of the time. By selectively reviewing the evidence, by creating magazines to publish your own supportive data (because no peer-reviewed journal would accept it as unbiased), and by controlling the design of the evaluation and the implementation of your favorite method, material, or program, almost anyone can create the impression that "research shows" positive effects for their product or pedagogy.

Ideally, research studies would demonstrate the longer-term impact of interventions as well as report the shorter-term effects. Unfortunately, rather few studies report effects over periods greater than one year and many report the effects after only a few months. Longer-term studies are more complicated and more expensive but they are also essential.

In education we have no federal agency charged with examining the quality of educational methods, materials, or programs. No one runs "crash-dummy" tests on new materials, no one does skid-pad brake tests, no one checks the ingredients lists. This may be just as well. But it does mean that in the educational marketplace the buyer must truly beware! And there is a huge educational marketplace and incredible sums of money to be made in convincing administrators and teachers to buy your educational stuff (including this book and my consulting services).

There is one final problem with research available today. In most cases, the available studies evaluated the effects of a literacy intervention on assessments of "basic literacy," not on "thoughtful literacy" assessments. In other words, most studies, especially the older studies, used word lists, tests of sub-skill knowledge, or assessments of low-level comprehension found on traditional standardized tests with their multiple-choice items. Thus, we have only a handful of studies that have evaluated interventions against student attainment of the new, higher-order literacy standards. But it is against student achievement of these new, higher standards that schools are typically now being evaluated.

For years, no one actually paid much attention to "research" evidence on various methods, materials, and programs. Yes, marketing departments often created some flyer or glossy designed to convince the occasionally wary buyer that there was a research base for the product. And none of this is to suggest that research did not influence the design of educational methods, materials, and products—it did. But today there are greater demands on publishers and promoters to have actual research on the effects the implementation has had on the achievement of students. This is different from being able to point to studies that influenced the design of your method, material, or program—the more traditional test. So, why the demand for research evidence now?

The Reading Excellence Act

The Reading Excellence Act (REA) was signed into law in the fall of 1998. The REA is the latest federal effort to reshape American reading instruction, in this case by setting criteria for the sorts of instructional practices that might be supported with federal funds and establishing a review process to better monitor how federal funds are used. The REA represents the most recent shift in restricting local educational decision-making. In other words, while federal funds have always had some controls on how they might be used, the REA substantially increases those restrictions.

The restrictions are set primarily in the requirement that federal monies allocated under this Act fund only instructional practices supported by "scientifically based reading research." The REA guidelines define such research. (See the following section.) These nonregulatory guidelines extensively detail what research is to be considered "scientifically based" research. Earlier, the federal Comprehensive School Reform Demonstration Program had required that funded programs be based on evidence of (a) a theoretical or research foundation, (b) improvements in student achievement, and (c) replicability (the project has previously been successfully implemented in more than one school). The REA expands on this by providing greater detail in defining just what sort of research is to be considered in verifying the effects of a method, material, or program.

It would be difficult to oppose the design of research-based instructional programs. But, as mentioned earlier, the research available does not provide a blueprint for effective instructional programs. Further, the sort of research base envisioned in the REA is difficult, if not impossible, to construct. So bear with me as we look at the several REA criteria for "scientifically based" reading research and examine the implications in terms of local decision making about reading instruction (the following section is drawn directly from the REA website: *www.ed.gov/inits/FY99/REAguidance/sectionB.html*).

REA: SCIENTIFICALLY BASED READING RESEARCH

What is Scientifically Based Reading Research?

The statute defines scientifically based reading research as the application of rigorous, systematic, and objective procedures to obtain valid knowledge relevant to reading development, reading instruction, and reading difficulties (Section 2252(5)). To meet the statutory definition, the research must:

- employ systematic, empirical methods that draw on observation or experiment;
- involve rigorous data analyses that are adequate to test the stated hypotheses and justify the general conclusions drawn;

- rely on measurements or observational methods that provide valid data across evaluators and observers and across multiple measurements and observations; and
- have been accepted by a peer-reviewed journal or approved by a panel of independent experts through a comparably rigorous, objective, and scientific review.

What are Characteristics of Scientifically Based Reading Research?

When reviewing research findings to determine whether the research met the four criteria specified in the REA (listed in bold below), readers may want to ask themselves questions about how well any particular study meets each of the criteria. Examples of the types of questions that could be asked about each criteria include:

- **Use of rigorous, systematic, and empirical methods.** Does the work have a solid theoretical or research foundation? Was it carefully designed to avoid biased findings and unwarranted claims of effectiveness? Does the research clearly delineate how the research was conducted, by whom it was conducted, and on whom it was conducted? Does it explain what procedures were followed to avoid spurious findings?
- **Adequacy of the data analyses to test the stated hypotheses and justify the general conclusions drawn.** Was the research designed to minimize alternative explanations for observed effects? Are the observed effects consistent with the overall conclusions and claims of effectiveness? Does the research present convincing documentation that the observed results were the result of the intervention? Does the research make clear what populations were studied (i.e., does it describe the participants' ages, as well as their demographic, cognitive, academic, and behavioral characteristics), and does it describe to whom the findings can be generalized? Does the study provide a full description of the outcome measures?
- **Reliance on measurements or observational methods that provided valid data across evaluators and observers and across multiple measurements and observations.** Are the findings based on a single-investigator single-classroom study, or were similar findings observed by multiple investigators in numerous locations? What procedures were in place to minimize researcher biases? Do observed results "hold up" over time? Are the study interventions described in sufficient detail to allow for replicability? Does the research explain how instructional fidelity was ensured and assessed?
- **Acceptance by a peer-reviewed journal or approved by a panel of independent experts through a comparably rigorous, objective, and scientific review.**

Has the research been carefully reviewed by unbiased individuals who were not part of the research study? Have the findings been subjected to external scrutiny and verification?

Thinking About the REA Guidelines. The first guideline focuses on the *use of rigorous, systematic, and empirical methods* in the design of the study, which is not particularly surprising. After all, research has been, traditionally, an empirical adventure. But several potential problems are created here. For instance, if a program developer closely monitors the implementation and the evaluation, is there an unintended biasing effect? In other words, would program developers pay more attention to implementation detail than an independent evaluator or the professional staff of a school district that also decided to implement the program and gauge its effects? My guess is that, yes, probably the developer would pay more attention. If so, are the effects the developer achieves reliable? That is, can they be achieved by others? Realize that the added attention the developer pays to implementation may not come from any ego- or profit-driven motive but, rather, from a clearer understanding of just how the program is supposed to work. If the program involves providing specific training to the teachers involved, can any two staff development providers actually offer identical training? And what if the teachers at your site are less experienced and have larger classes than the teachers at the developer's site? The point here is that "rigorous and systematic" methods often have to be adapted from site to site. A "teacher is a teacher is a teacher" just isn't true any more than suggesting that classrooms and schools are all largely comparable.

The difficulty in designing rigorous, systematic research studies in real schools is typified in the armful of "adequacy" reviews that have been published (e.g., Coles, 2000; Lysynchuk et al.,1989; Pressley & Allington, 1999; Swanson & Hoskyn, 1999; Troia, 1998). These reviews share a single common feature. They all note how few published studies meet the rigorous and systematic criteria set forth in the REA. Swanson and Hoskyn (1998), for instance, reviewed over 900 studies of instructional interventions with children identified as learning disabled. Of these studies, only 180 met minimal criteria for rigor and less than 10 percent were rated as exhibiting high-quality research methodology. Troia (1999) reviewed 39 studies of phonemic awareness interventions and noted that fewer than a quarter met even two-thirds of the criteria of rigorously designed research.

Much of the messiness in educational research stems from the problem of achieving purely random assignment of subjects. It would be difficult, if not impossible, to approach a school system and ask for participation in a research study that required all teachers and children to be randomly assigned to buildings across the district. But without such random assignment it is impossible to control for school, teacher, and community effects that might bias the outcome. In virtually all funded research, both teachers and children (actually their parents) must volunteer to participate. What of the teachers who don't volunteer? Are they "comparable" to the volunteers? In other words, would not including these teachers bias the results? Would teachers who were better teachers be more likely to volunteer? That would likely bias the effect of the intervention in a positive direction. Would parents of higher-achieving students be more likely to return permission slips than parents of lower-achieving students? That would also create a positive bias. Do some schools have a larger supply of better teachers? Or a larger number of low-achieving children?

In order to conduct a "true experiment," researchers must attempt to eliminate such bias in their subject sample. Random selection is the historical strategy for eliminating such bias. In true random assignment every teacher or student or classroom is randomly selected from the population to either participate in the intervention or to serve as a "control" participant. The control participants do not receive the special treatment. But as anyone who works in schools knows all too well, getting teachers and parents to agree to random assignment to schools and classrooms is simply not feasible. Even getting schools to randomly assign students within a building has not been easy and that doesn't address the issue of possible teacher bias.

Think of the issue another way. If you wanted to achieve the best effects from an intervention, wouldn't selecting the interested volunteer teachers as the intervention teachers be desirable? And that is just what most schools (and many researchers) do when they field test an intervention. But in a rigorous research study, such biased selection would violate this first principle. At the same time, following federal human subject protection guidelines, required for virtually all federally funded studies, means that participating teachers provide "informed consent." In other words, teachers must be informed about the study and have the opportunity to decline to participate. We should not be surprised that teachers who see the proposed intervention in a more favorable light are more likely to volunteer. Thus, it seems that much research presents a "best case" scenario—which is how the intervention works when teachers volunteer to try it.

Participating in an unbiased research study can create public relations problems for a school district. Consider, for instance, the sorts of parental concerns that could arise even with no random assignment of teachers. If some children are randomly selected to participate in an early reading intervention, say, and other children with similar needs are selected to be the unserved control students, parents of this latter group will undoubtedly object to this lack of services. Or if some randomly selected children receive a tutorial intervention and other similar children are assigned to work in a small group with a paraprofessional, parents can object and with reason. Also imagine how much more difficult the situation becomes when some classrooms are offering the special program while others are not.

Rigorous, unbiased scientific research is an ivory tower standard that is just very hard to accomplish in the real world of schools, teachers, and children.

The second guideline asks whether *the data analyses were adequate to test the stated hypotheses and justify the general conclusions drawn.* In an ideal world, every study would have a randomly selected group of teachers and children who received the experimental intervention and another randomly selected group of teachers and children who did not. Everything about the instruction offered would be identical except one group would participate in the intervention and the other would not. The question is, when do we fit the intervention in if instruction is to be otherwise comparable? Would some children simply stay in school longer each day? That doesn't work because then we couldn't decide whether it was the intervention instructional design or just adding more instruction, regardless of the type, that led to any observed achievement effects.

However, participating in a special project has been observed to raise scores even if no real intervention is offered. This has been dubbed the *Hawthorne Effect*. This effect was first noticed in a manufacturing plant in Hawthorne, NJ, many years ago. Workers there were more productive when they were told they were being studied as part of a special project even though no actual experiment was conducted. To guard against the "added instruction" and Hawthorne effects, rigorous research design typically attempts to provide some other special intervention to the control group but an intervention thought not to have any real impact on, say, reading achievement.

So, a researcher might add a reading tutorial to the daily schedule of a group of randomly selected lower-achieving readers to assess its effects. At the same time, another group of randomly selected lower-achieving readers would receive a handwriting tutorial. In this case, the Hawthorne Effect is effectively nullified. Both groups of children receive a tutorial. But the "added instruction" problem still exists. One group received additional reading instruction, the other didn't. So why would anyone be surprised if the students receiving the added reading instruction had higher reading achievement at the end of the study?

To counter the added instruction problem, the researcher might offer two types of tutorials both targeted at reading improvement. In one case the children might be tutored with an emphasis on developing decoding strategies—offered an Alphabetic Phonics tutorial. The other group might receive a different focus, perhaps reading fluency training with an emphasis on rereading texts until a certain fluency level has been achieved. In such cases, both the Hawthorne and added instruction problems are fairly effectively countered, assuming that both groups of students and their tutors were randomly selected. If the children participating in one of the tutoring interventions record higher achievement at the end of the year (and perhaps for years to come), then with such a design it would be possible to consider that the observed effects were neither biased nor chance differences but real achievement differences attributable to differences in the effectiveness of the interventions.

But what happens if the effectiveness of the intervention is measured on a test of the ability to pronounce nonsense syllables? Does the selection of that outcome measure bias the outcome? Would significantly higher scores on a nonsense word test suggest that the decoding intervention was more effective—at fostering improved reading achievement? What if the outcome measure was a test of reading fluency? Is a test of fluency a more appropriate test of reading achievement than a test of nonsense word pronunciation? Would a test of fluency be biased toward the fluency intervention? How about a test of spelling? Or retelling of narrative read silently? What if the decoding intervention improved nonsense word pronunciation but had no effect on fluency and the fluency treatment produced the opposite result? Would such a finding be unexpected?

Thus, how the effects of an intervention are evaluated makes a huge difference in conclusions about effectiveness. This is an important issue because one criticism of much of the intervention research focused on developing decoding skills is that while there are reported effects on nonsense word pronunciation these studies less often reported positive effects on other assessments of reading achievement (Allington & Woodside-Jiron, 1999; Lyon & Moats, 1997; Pressley & Allington, 1999). In other words, many phonics interventions demonstrate improved pronunciation of nonsense words but no improvement in real reading achievement (e.g., reading fluency and comprehension).

There are also concerns about what sort of reading assessment was used—experimenter-developed, nonstandardized commercial batteries, or standardized commercial assessments? Swanson and Hoskyn (1998) reported that the studies they reviewed that used standardized assessments of reading routinely produced smaller gains than the studies that reported results on experimenter-developed tests and tests of subskills. In other words, it is easier to design a study that produces narrow achievement effects, especially on experimenter-developed assessments, than a study that produces broader effects on standardized assessments. But that shouldn't be surprising. However, it should be a concern when considering the effects of any intervention.

Another issue to consider here is the size of the effect observed. Historically, tests of statistical significance have been used to estimate the reliability of differences in achievement between groups. But a test of statistical significance only tells us that observed differences did not occur by chance, regardless of how small that difference is. So, with a large enough sample of students, even small differences in achievement can turn out to be statistically significant. But when do such differences become educationally significant?

Venezky (1998) reported on a reanalysis of the reading achievement in schools that had adopted the Success for All program. The research on SFA had shown statistically significant effects on reading achievement (Slavin et al., 1993). But Venezky noted that fifth-grade students in SFA schools had average reading achievement grade levels of 3.6 while the students in the control schools had a 3.2 average reading level. The four-month difference in reading achievement was statistically significant but Venezky asked whether—after six years of an intervention—such a difference was educationally significant. Or cost-effective. He suggested that it seemed less important that intervention results be compared statistically to control groups and more important that interventions also be evaluated against a fixed standard: how many students achieved the state standards, achieved grade-level performance, became avid, voluntary readers.

Finally, it is important to consider the generalizability of the results. Does the population in the study represent the diversity of teachers and students found in American schools? This is, of course, a standard that would be almost impossible to achieve in a single research project. Nevertheless, it is a useful question to consider. If the study was conducted in New York state, where all teachers must earn a master's degree within three to five years and your school is located in a state with less rigorous standards for teachers (and perhaps many teachers working with emergency credentials), can the results be generalized from one location to another? If the teachers who implemented the intervention were volunteers, can we expect the same effects from teachers who were mandated to implement an intervention? If the study was conducted in a school located in an upper-middle-class suburb can the results be generalized to schools in any neighborhood? What if the study school had a 20–1 student-teacher ratio and your school has a 28–1 ratio? Generalizability rests, in large part, on comparability of populations—both students and teachers. Without rich information on the community, the teachers, the school context, and the students, it is difficult to judge comparability. And when such information is provided, it is often difficult to locate studies with comparable populations that would allow generalization from one site to another.

The third guideline asks whether the researcher *relied on measurements or observational methods that provided valid data across evaluators and observers and across multiple measurements and observations.* This could be considered a "fidelity of implementation" guideline. Did the researcher provide evidence that the intervention was actually implemented? Did observers monitor implementation? Was the effectiveness of the intervention related to quality of the implementation? Consider, for instance, the case of California. Almost simultaneously schools in California were provided funds to 1) reduce class size in the primary grades, 2) provide primary grade teachers with staff development on teaching phonics, and 3) provide new "phonics-emphasis" curriculum materials. How might a researcher sort out the separate effects of these three different, but simultaneously enacted reforms?

There actually is almost no way one could attribute improved achievement to any of the three reforms without some careful observation of the staff development provided and the instruction offered before and after participation in the staff development.

In other words, to attribute achievement changes to participating in the staff development intervention, you would have to be able to document how classroom instruction changed after the staff development and then link those changes to improved student achievement. If some teachers' instruction changed substantially and others did not, then you might expect some children to have substantial gains and others to make modest improvements, if any. In such a case, claims linking improved achievement to participation in the staff development could be reasonably made. Now, if the changes in instruction involved a greater frequency of the use of the new phonics materials, then perhaps claims could be made about their influence. But there is still the problem of estimating the effects of the class-size reduction reform. Smaller classes produce better achievement even without professional development or new curriculum materials of whatever ilk.

Note that in this example there is no control group per se. All teachers participated in the staff development. Judgments about the link between staff development and improved achievement are supported by linking differential implementation to differential patterns of achievement growth. Finding any such studies, however, is enormously difficult. This may be because of the expense involved in having observers in classrooms both before and after participation. It may be because policy makers rarely produce policies that are easily studied. Or it may be because policy makers seem rarely interested in evidence of the effects of their policy making (Allington, 2000). Rather, when it comes time for a reelection campaign they just assert that their favorite policy was the basis for any improvements observed (with no evidence, scientific or otherwise to support the assertion).

So far we have not considered the problem of ensuring that different observers actually observe and record the same teaching behaviors in the same ways. This is called "interrater reliability." In other words, two raters watching the same lesson would rate it very nearly identically on some observational scale. Similarly, we haven't discussed constructing an observational system that has been shown to focus on the key features of instruction—the features that produce the higher achievement. More often than not, research studies that include a monitoring of the fidelity of implementation fall short on these two criteria: demonstrations of interrater reliability and demonstrations of the predictive validity of the observational scale.

Now all of this seems overly technical and more than a bit nit-picky. But consider the claims of effectiveness that have been made for any number of methods, materials, and programs and then consider the evidence available to support those claims. Truth be told, it is difficult to find evidence that meets the REA criteria for virtually any educational innovation. That shouldn't be surprising since even the much-lauded medical research—often held up as the ideal for education—has suffered through charges that much of the research available used only men as subjects. Or used populations that underrepresented minorities, people living in poverty, and people living in rural regions. Or for excluding the obviously healthy in their samples. Or for being potentially biased because the funding for the research came from the drug company marketing the treatment. And the recent flurry of contradictory medical research on the role of salt in one's diet, the utility of mammograms, the benefits of red wine, and so on, points to the difficulty that even medical science has in delivering "rigorous, reliable scientific research" that achieves consensus findings.

Far too much educational intervention research falls short on the fidelity of implementation criteria. That is, few studies actually even attempt to estimate whether the intervention was effectively implemented. The combination of the cost of such a demonstration and the lack of demand for such evidence both work to create an environment whereby it is asserted that an intervention was implemented and then assertions about the effects, or the lack of them, are also made. In order to understand the effects of an intervention it is necessary to gather information on its implementation. This seems especially true in education where any number of studies have shown that rather few features of any intervention ever studied were actually implemented as imagined by the developer and few of the implemented changes survived over the longer term (McGill-Franzen, 2000).

The final guideline proposed in the REA suggests that when papers reporting research on method, materials and programs have gained *acceptance through publication in a peer-reviewed journal or approved by a panel of independent experts through a comparably rigorous, objective, and scientific review*, more confidence can be placed in the findings. I agree. But this is hardly a fail-proof test. Consider that the majority of the studies reviewed by Lysynchuk et al., (1989); Pressley and Allington (1999); Swanson and Hoskyn (1998); and Troia (1999) were published in peer reviewed journals. Yet typically fewer than a half of the published studies reviewed met the minimum quality standards set by the authors. Suffice it to say that there are many published, but poorly designed, studies in the educational literature.

Part of the reason for this has been alluded to above. It is darn difficult and, typically, expensive, to design and carry out well-designed educational intervention research. Given how financial support for educational research has eroded over the past thirty years and how few school districts or state education agencies or publishers actually fund any research on methods, materials, or programs, no one should be surprised that far too many educational research projects cut corners (and costs) in ways that impact on the quality of the results—at least in terms of the confidence we can place in the reliability and generalizability of the results.

In addition, every year more educational journals and magazines appear in the marketplace. These magazines need articles to fill their pages. Thus, the past thirty years have seen a veritable explosion of journals that seem willing to accept reports of lower and lower quality research. In a similar vein, fewer of the journals and magazines now insist on peer review. And relatively few journals can be considered high-quality research publications where the peers doing the review are established and recognized educational researchers. Too many educational publications, in my view, exhibit precisely the opposite attitude to educational articles as that exhibited by the popular media. While the popular media seems to focus almost exclusively on "bad news" stories about

---

High-Quality Educational Research Journals

There are, literally, a hundred or more journals and magazines that publish educational research. However, there are but a handful of journals that require rigorous peer review. While no list can be comprehensive, below are my nominees for the journals most likely to publish high-quality studies or reviews of research:

Review of Educational Research	*Journal of Literacy Research*
American Educational Research Journal	*Child Development*
Journal of Educational Research	*Reading Research Quarterly*
Journal of Educational Psychology	*Issues in Education*

education, educational magazines and journals focus primarily on good news stories. Think about the educational magazines and journals you read. How many articles in these publications reported on the failure of a reform or an intervention?

SUMMARY

It is important, I believe, that educators become better informed and more critical of claims of educational effects—positive or negative. As a profession we need to become more skillful at reading the promotional claims and the research assertions for educational interventions. I think we need to become more informed consumers of methods, materials, and programs. Claims of effectiveness will increase geometrically now that "research-based" instruction sits in the spotlight. But every claim needs to be examined with a skeptic's eye while applying the general guidelines promoted by the REA.

Let me offer one example. Currently, many claims of effectiveness are being made for one particular reading series. The proponents of the series suggest that it is a phonics emphasis with the accompanying use of "decodable" texts that makes this program effective. But when we were studying school programs several years ago, we noted that this reading series occupied almost twice as much instructional time each day as its competitors. Now knowing that there is a long-established link between "time-on-task" and achievement (Denham & Lieberman, 1980), one might suspect that any achievement effects observed might also be attributed, in some part, to the fact that more time was spent on reading instruction in classrooms using that series. But there seem to be no studies that, while comparing this series to another, observed and analyzed the actual lesson times allocated to each series. Now it could be that the phonics component is the real reason for the report of higher achievement in schools using this series. But without instructional time data we will never know.

It should also be noted that the single study reporting a modest positive effect for using this series has been criticized on several design and analysis features (Coles, 2000; Pressley & Allington, 1999; Taylor, 1998). Each of these critiques raise fundamental questions about the reliability of the conclusions drawn by the researchers in reporting this study, although none seriously raise the issue of time allocated to reading lessons.

Likewise, since there has been not a single study that systematically manipulated the use of decodable texts—texts where almost all the words are pronounceable given the letter-sound associations that have been taught—including studies examining the effectiveness of this series (Allington & Woodside-Jiron, 1998; Pressley & Allington, 1999; Taylor, 1998). Claims about the utility of decodable texts are sheer nonsense and not supported by the research available. But this lack of research has not inhibited proponents of a more code-emphasis–or phonics emphasis–curriculum. Indeed, several states have now mandated the use of decodable texts and in each case assert, incorrectly, that their policies are "research-based."

All of this may lead you to think that educational research is not going to be very helpful in designing higher-quality reading instruction.

But you would be wrong. We have learned an enormous amount about the characteristics of more effective reading programs and more effective reading instruction. To use these findings, however, you have to move beyond the current fixation on methods, materials, and programs. When we ask about which method, material, or program is most effective, we ask a question that, literally, cannot be answered by referring to the research. As noted throughout this chapter, virtually every method, material, and program has accumulated some evidence that "it works!" But the evidence is often contradicted by other evidence. And the quality of the evidence, using the REA guidelines, is often dismal, at best.

In designing more effective reading instruction, we will need to look to the research for larger issues than answers to questions about particular methods, materials, and programs. There seems a simple, but often overlooked reason for this. The search for any "one best way" to teach children is doomed to fail because it is a search for the impossible (Cunningham & Allington, 1999).

A simple principle—Children differ—explains why there can be no one best method, material, or program. This simple principle has been reaffirmed so repeatedly in educational research that one would think that folks would have noticed it by now. In addition, anyone who grew up with siblings or who has more than one child of their own, knows from powerful experience that no two children are alike. Not even those from the same family gene pool. What then to make of a classroom with twenty-four children from forty-eight sets of pooled genes?

A corollary principle—Teachers differ—has been largely ignored as well even though, again, we have lots of research evidence on the issue. In other words, no teachers are exactly the same. We've learned just how hard it is to get teachers to teach "against the grain": To teach in ways that contradict their beliefs and understandings about teaching, learning, and reading and writing. If you want an intervention to fail, mandate its use with a school full of teachers who hate it, don't agree with, and are not skilled (or planning to become skilled) in using it. This is what Linda Darling-Hammond (1990) has called "the power of the bottom over the top" in educational reform.

In any school, then, you have a horde of students who differ in innumerable ways and a cluster of teachers who also differ in a myriad of ways. Expecting any single method, material, or program to work equally well with every kid in every classroom is nonsensical. And yet we see increasing pressure for a standardization of reading curriculum and lessons in the expectation that this will improve outcomes. The substantial research evidence that such plans have not produced the desired effects is routinely ignored in the latest quest for a cheap, quick fix (Duffy & Hoffman, 1999).

In the remainder of this book, I attempt to address some of the lunacy of the current reading reform movement. Because the REA has set such a visible standard for using research to redesign reading instruction, I have attempted to develop a research-based argument for how we might best use what we

---

The 100/100 Goal.

Imagine that we could design schools where 100% of the students were involved in instruction appropriate to their needs and development 100% of the day. Imagine how different the achievement patterns of struggling readers might be. I will suggest that the 100/100 goal is, perhaps, the real solution for developing schools that better serve struggling readers.

---

have learned (from research) in the redesign of reading instruction in American schools.

This book focuses on the converging evidence that is available on the features of reading that really matter. I leave to others to debate particular methods, materials, and programs. In this book I develop a research-based framework for rethinking reading instruction generally, and particularly the reading instruction that we offer kids who struggle while learning to read.

WHAT REALLY MATTERS: KIDS NEED TO READ A LOT

Everyone has heard the proverb: Practice makes perfect. In learning to read it is true that reading practice—just reading—is a powerful contributor to the development of accurate, fluent, high-comprehension reading. In fact, if I were required to select a single aspect of the instructional environment to change, my first choice would be creating a schedule that supported dramatically increased quantities of reading during the school day. What evidence has convinced me of the essential need for such change? Where would I start the change process? What would the school day look like if such a change were achieved?

RESEARCH ON VOLUME OF READING

How Much Reading is Enough Reading?

This is one of those unanswerable questions because children differ. It is also a difficult question because the answer would depend, at least in part, on what kind of readers you were satisfied with. Think of it this way. If you think most American kids read well enough now, then maybe not much more reading is needed (and given second in the world ranking perhaps your conclusion is right). But if you were disturbed by the fact that few American students seem to read with high levels of higher-order understanding, then perhaps you would argue for more reading since the evidence available suggests that volume is linked to attaining the higher-order literacy proficiencies. Or maybe you would argue for more reading just for the kids whose progress remains somewhat below a level you find satisfactory. Those children identified as learning disabled, for instance. Or maybe you are more upset by the fact that the amount of reading kids do declines as they go through school and you would redesign the middle- and secondary school programs so that adolescents were expected to read more in school. Finally, you might not even care so much about how kids' reading stacks up on international or national assessments but be dismayed that rather few children, especially adolescents, engage in much free voluntary reading (Krashen, 1993). In other words, you may be more concerned with reading habits than with reading achievement per se and hope that we might create instructional environments that resulted in more children, adolescents, and, ultimately, adults who were more inclined to read.

How you think about American reading achievement and reading habits will influence what you perceive as an appropriate response to the question: How much reading is enough? (We will get to the question: What kind of reading? a bit later in the book). There is no evidence that suggests *precisely* how much or how often children and adolescents need to read to develop high levels of reading proficiency. There are only a handful of experimental studies where increasing the quantity of reading was the primary intervention. But Krashen (1993) notes that in 93 percent of the reading comprehension test comparisons students who were assigned more reading or allocated more reading time in school performed as well or better than students who did not have the added reading assigned or that added time allocated. In the nine studies that were of a year or more duration, eight found positive achievement effects, one found no significant difference, and no studies found an achievement advantage for students in the traditional, control classes. In other words, replacing whatever went on in classrooms with added reading time was just as effective as, or more effective than, traditional instruction in enhancing reading comprehension performance.

But half of the studies reviewed by Krashen were published between 1940 and 1969, with the majority of the remaining studies published in the 1970s and 1980s. Now there is absolutely nothing wrong with older studies, in fact too often we seem to ignore much of what educational research found in the past. But the older studies do raise a number of potential questions about the generalizability of the findings to schools today. Especially given the new thoughtful literacy standards. In addition, the published intervention studies suffer from many of the weaknesses that seem almost inherent in classroom-based intervention research. But there is more recent evidence also available. Much of this other evidence is contrastive, correlational, or explanatory.

Contrastive Studies.   In these studies the volume of reading done by higher- and lower-achieving readers has been well documented. In a series of studies I reported that differences in the volume of classroom reading were associated with elementary students' reading achievement (Allington, 1977; 1980; 1983; 1984; Allington & McGill-Franzen, 1989). In these studies, the average higher-achieving student read approximately three times as much each week as their lower-achieving classmates. These differences did not include out-of-school voluntary reading. Likewise, Collins (1986) reported on first-grade instruction noting that the higher-achieving students spent approximately 70 percent of their instructional time reading passages and discussing or responding to questions about the material they read. By way of contrast, the lower-achieving readers spent roughly half as much time on these activities (37 percent), with word identification drill, letter-sound activities, and spelling and penmanship activities occupying large blocks of lesson time. Thus, contrastive studies of classroom experiences consistently indicate that lower-achieving readers simply read less during the school day than their higher-achieving peers, spending more instructional time on other activities.

But there is another reason for the discrepancy in the volume of reading. Lower-achieving students are more often reported to be reading aloud, usually reading aloud to their teacher in a small group setting (Allington, 1983; Hiebert, 1983). When children read aloud, only one child is necessarily reading (although other children might be following along or reading ahead). In contrast, during silent reading, each reader reads. Thus, in a small group engaged in oral reading each of the four children might only read 100 words while the children in the same group engaged in silent reading would read 400 words. Since oral reading is slower and because various interruptions are more likely to occur, it may be the case that children would read more than 400 words silently given the same time period as it takes for four students to each read 100 words of text aloud in a traditional round-robin reading format.

Other contrastive studies have examined the volume of reading done by higher- and lower-achieving readers in and out of school. The classic study was conducted by Anderson, Wilson, and Fielding (1988). In this study fifth-grade students kept reading logs documenting their out-of-school reading. Again, the findings illustrated the enormous differences in volume of reading between higher- and lower-achieving students. Figure 2.1 illustrates just how large the differences in reading volume would be across a year's period of time.

Nagy and Anderson (1984) estimated that differences in the volume of in-school reading would also be substantial with some middle-grade children reading as few as 100,000 words a year, the average student reading about 1,000,000 per year, and the voracious middle grade readers reading over 10,000,000 words per year. They argued that given the known power of wide reading in developing children's vocabulary knowledge, such differences provide powerful explanatory evidence for differences in student vocabulary growth and vocabulary size.

Correlational Studies.   The most recent correlational evidence for the positive effects of extensive reading on reading achievement can be found in the *1998 NAEP Reading Report Card for the Nation* (U.S. Department of Education, 1999; also available at http://nces.ed.gov/naep). At every age level, reading more

Figure 2.1
Reading Volume of Fifth-grader Students of Different Levels of Achievement
Adapted from Anderson, Wilson and Fielding, 1988.

Achievement percentile	Minutes of reading per day	Words per year
90th	40.4	2,357,000
50th	12.9	601,000
10th	1.6	51,000

pages in school and for homework each day was associated with higher reading scores. The NAEP report notes, "There is a consistent relationship between the amount of reading done in school and for homework and the students' scale scores" (p. 88). At each grade level, then, students who read more pages each day were more likely to achieve the Proficient level of performance on the NAEP reading assessment. For instance, at twelfth grade, only 28 percent of students who reported reading five or fewer pages each day achieved the Proficient level compared to 51 percent of those students who read eleven or more pages. But while students reported reading more pages each day than was reported by students on previous NAEP administrations, fewer than half of the eighth and twelfth graders report reading eleven or more pages each day (though more than half of fourth-grade students read that many pages).

Foertsch (1992) examined the background factors that were most closely related to reading instruction and reading performance on the NAEP, including instructional approaches, reading experiences, home influences, and demographic characteristics. Data for these analyses were collected from a nationally representative sample of approximately 13,000 students in 1988 and 25,000 students in 1990 at grades 4, 8, and 12 attending public and private schools.

The major findings were: (1) the amount of reading that students do in and out of school was positively related to their reading achievement, yet most students report relatively little reading in or out of school; (2) despite extensive research suggesting that effective reading instruction includes moving from an emphasis on workbooks to lessons that offer more extensive reading and writing activities, many children still spent inordinate amounts of time on workbook activities (which had no positive relationship with reading achievement; (3) students who reported home environments that fostered reading activity had higher reading achievement; and (4) students demonstrated difficulty in providing details and arguments to support interpretations of what they read. The nature of the more effective reading environments seems consistent with other reports of highly effective reading instruction in its emphasis on engaging children and adolescents in substantive volume of reading and writing about that reading on a daily basis.

Correlational studies such as the NAEP report do not provide evidence of a causal link between greater quantities of reading and higher achievement. But correlational evidence of this sort—large-scale, nationally representative student sample, well-designed thoughtful literacy assessment—cannot be disregarded. The NAEP is simply the largest and most comprehensive set of

---

Improving American Reading Achievement

"Surveys conducted as part of the National Assessment of Educational Progress suggest the simplest of all solutions [for fostering improved reading]: Encourage and challenge children to read."

(*Education Week*, February 17, 1999, p. 16)

correlational data demonstrating the link between reading volume and reading achievement.

Other correlational studies have explored the relationship between extensive reading and reading proficiency in children and adults. McQuillan (1998) provides a summary of a number of such studies including seven studies that examined this relationship in English-speaking children and adults. In each case these studies employed author and/or title recognition checklists to estimate how much reading experience varied from person to person. While Taylor (1998) has offered substantial criticisms about the adequacy of such measures in reliably reflecting reading experience, these studies have produced consistent findings showing positive correlations between the measures of reading activity and reading comprehension and vocabulary development.

Two of these studies reported on the relationship between reading volume and school-aged children's reading comprehension. Cipielewski and Stanovich (1992) found that individual differences in reading comprehension growth were reliably linked to differences in print exposure—volume of reading—even when decoding skills were accounted for in the analyses. McBride-Chang et al. (1993) also found that volume of reading was reliably correlated with reading comprehension performance in both disabled and normally achieving readers. Elley (1992) reported a strong positive relationship between teacher reports of time allocated to silent reading in their classrooms and reading comprehension proficiency of their students, this across an international sample of schools.

Correlational evidence is suggestive. The available data suggest that, at the very least, more reading generally accompanies improved reading. Some would argue a stronger link: More reading produces better reading. But correlational data don't answer the "chicken and egg" problem (Does better reading lead to more reading? Or does more reading lead to better reading?). Other sorts of studies do address this issue.

Explanatory Studies.   There are several sorts of studies that illuminate the question of the link between volume and proficiency of reading. The well-proven impact of time-on-task (Fisher & Berliner, 1985) seems to account for much of the relationship between volume of reading and achievement. The research on Academic Learning Time (ALT)—the time students spend actively engaged in academic learning tasks with high levels of success—yielded consistently positive relationships between ALT and achievement over a remarkably broad range of ages and subjects (Berliner, 1981). These research findings were found to be so commonsensical that many have trivialized this work and too many have, seemingly, ignored the potential implications for the design of reading instruction. In other words, most educators were not surprised to find that time spent in academic engagement in double tasks was related to improved achievement. Nor were many surprised that different types of tasks (e.g., worksheets, question answering, silent reading, flash card drill, Go Fish phonics games) produced different sorts of achievement gains and had different effects on broad measures of reading proficiency (Stallings, 1980). But today

Correlational Evidence is Important

At the annual meeting of the International Reading Association in Indianapolis in May, 2000, Jim Cunningham, of the University of North Carolina—Chapel Hill raised an interesting point. He questioned the National Reading Panel's downplaying of the substantial correlational evidence between extensive reading and reading achievement by noting that the tobacco lobbyists made precisely the same arguments about the studies linking smoking and lung cancer. That is, the numerous consistent and long-term studies demonstrating a correlation between cigarette smoking and lung cancer didn't prove that cigarettes *caused* that cancer. Nonetheless, that argument failed to keep the Surgeon General from requiring warnings on cigarette packages and the tobacco companies from agreeing, in an out-of-court settlement, to provide billions of dollars to states as compensation for lung cancer costs. Perhaps workbooks and all skill-and-drill reproducibles should be required to carry a warning: Caution. Sustained use of this product may cause reading/learning difficulties. Conversely books might carry a label that said: Research has demonstrated that regular reading of this product can reduce the risks of acquiring a reading/learning disability.

much of that early groundbreaking work on learning to read in classrooms seems to have been forgotten in current educational reform initiatives.

For instance, with all the activity around developing educational standards, few states or school districts seem to have developed standards for volume of reading. One exception is New York State where the English Language Arts standards require that twenty-five books be read per year. This extensive reading standard, as it is called, is an across-the-curriculum standard (as is the extensive writing standard of 1,000 words per month.) In other words, meeting these standards is the responsibility of all curriculum areas, not just the English or Language Arts teachers. Now I cannot say that I think that twenty-five books a year or 1,000 words of writing each month are good or bad standards in terms of adequate volume. Books vary on a number of dimensions that I think are important and simply establishing a number of books to be read seems to have several serious limitations. Likewise, I usually prefer shorter, better-written papers than longer badly crafted papers. Nonetheless, the New York standards do provide a clear basis for rethinking the curriculum plan in most schools, K–12. It may be that these standards were developed because of the evidence that indicates that school and classroom contexts typically influence reading and writing volume. Some of this influence seems related to what the instructional plan emphasizes as important academic work. When a state plan calls for extensive reading and writing, such an outcome seems more likely than if no such outcomes are present in the state curriculum framework.

The evidence available suggests that planning for volume of reading and writing may be necessary. Keisling (1978), for instance, analyzed the uses of instructional time in four school districts and found that classrooms in some districts routinely provided more time for reading and reading instruction and that these allocations were related to reading achievement. More instructional time for reading most consistently produced greater gains and achievement gains in lower-achieving students especially. But most districts were unaware that their allocations were different from those of other districts. Mervar and Hiebert (1989) documented substantial differences in the volume of reading recorded in schools using basal reader series and those using a literature-based framework. In the latter classrooms the students read roughly twice as many words per week as their counterparts in the basal classrooms. This was true of both higher- and lower-achieving students. We found substantial volume differences between classrooms in the same district and between the volume of reading children did in schools in different districts (Allington et al., 1996). These differences were linked to differences in beliefs about the importance of engaging children in actual reading.

> We assumed that how teachers structured the learning environment would make a difference in how their students spent their time, and how students spent their time would influence the level of reading proficiency they attained at the end of the academic year. The data confirmed this expectation.
>
> (Leinhardt, et al., 1981, p. 357)

Other research demonstrates both the variability in reading volume from classroom to classroom and the effects that such variation has on students' reading growth. Leinhardt, Zigmond, and Cooley (1981) studied the reading lessons offered to 105 primary-grade students identified as learning disabled. During the classroom observations reading activity was broken into two broad categories: direct reading, in which the child was actually reading letters, words, sentences, and stories; and indirect reading in which the child was engaged in activity assumed to be related to reading that is not actually reading (e.g., copying, circling, phonics drill, questions, directions, etc.). Also coded were other activities (e.g., waiting, management, off-task). The observations documented that kids spent substantially more time in lessons called reading than they did actually engaged in direct reading even though 85 percent of the children were on-task and engaged in their lessons at any given point in time. The observations also indicated that there were large variations in the volume of direct reading between students and these differences predicted large differences in reading development.

To better understand the relationship between direct reading and reading growth, the classroom data were analyzed using regression analysis and causal modeling. These analyses pointed to the explanatory power of direct silent reading time in predicting reading growth—neither oral reading volume nor indirect reading activity significantly influenced posttest reading performance. The analyses suggest that an increase of five minutes daily silent reading would be predicted to produce an additional month's growth on a standardized reading achievement test.

The observations also pointed to the importance of good teaching—modeling and demonstrating useful reading strategies. For instance, even very small increases in the amount of daily teacher demonstration produced improved reading achievement. But their observational data indicated that most teachers offered little useful instruction. Only one minute a day was observed, on average, of the teacher offering explanations or demonstrations of elements of reading, though about fourteen minutes a day were spent in providing general directions about assignments. We will return to this issue in chapter 5.

Leinhardt and her colleagues suggest that increasing the amount of silent reading volume is the most obvious strategy for improving reading achievement. They note that well over an hour each day was spent in waiting, transitions, management, and other activities that could easily be replaced by additional reading time.

However, Wilkinson and his colleagues (1988) reanalyzed the data from the Leinhardt et al. study using a more rigorous technique for controlling for the influence of initial student reading achievement. Their reanalysis, controlling for entry-level reading, reduced the effect of silent reading time on achievement substantially and suggested that oral reading time had a greater impact on achievement. They suggest that LD students in this study had comprehension difficulties that restricted the volume of silent reading for lowest achievers. Oral reading, they hypothesize, "by virtue of its requirement for an overt response, may have placed greater demands on students for participation" (p. 141). Wilkinson and his colleagues argued that the evidence of a superior effect for silent reading was not reliable, at least for the LD students in this study.

More recently, Taylor and her colleagues (1990) studied the relationship between volume and reading achievement of 165 fifth- and sixth-grade general education students. The design of this study accounted for the concerns raised in the reanalysis by Wilkinson and his colleagues (1988). The students averaged sixteen minutes per day of reading during their fifty-minute reading period and fifteen minutes of reading at home. In some classrooms students read twice as much during the same fifty-minute reading period as students in other classrooms (9.6 min vs. 18.7 min). Taylor and her colleagues demonstrated that the minutes of reading per day during reading period contributed significantly (R^2 .62) to individual reading achievement growth while time spent on home reading did not.

Morrow (1992) confirmed the causal relationship between reading volume and reading achievement in her experimental study. Her intervention focused on the impact of developing classroom books centers in urban schools and restructuring the school day such that time was allocated for student use of these centers, including time to read. Guthrie and his colleagues (1999) also found reading volume predicted reading comprehension in third-, fifth-, eighth-, and tenth-grade students, even when pupil factors such as past reading achievement, prior knowledge, and motivation were controlled statistically.

Finally, the research also provides evidence for what I consider one of the greatest failures of the federally funded Title I remedial reading and special education programs: Neither program reliably increased the volume of reading that children engaged in (Allington & McGill-Franzen, 1989; Haynes & Jenkins, 1986; O'Sullivan et al., (1990). This failure may explain the limited impact that both programs have had on accelerating the reading development of the children served (Puma et al., 1997). Simply put, children who received extraordinary instructional support from either program often had the volume of reading reduced rather than expanded as remedial and resource room lessons focused on other activities.

At this point, then, these studies offer a number of useful guidelines while leaving some details yet to be verified. It would seem that the consistency of the evidence concerning the relationship of volume of reading and reading achievement is surely strong enough to support recommending attention to reading volume as a central feature of the design of any intervention focused on improving reading achievement.

Given the rich research evidence on the relationship between reading achievement and volume of reading, and the limited impact that special pro-

This Moncure Elementary School (VA) checks out titles available in the school's Books for a Buck collection.

grams have had on the volume of reading of lower-achieving students, any restructuring of an educational support program designed to enhance the reading development of children and adolescents—and to accelerate the literacy development of lower-achieving children especially—must start by considering the issue of volume of reading.

THINKING ABOUT VOLUME OF READING

So where do you begin in planning an intervention designed to enhance reading development of all children, but especially those children who now struggle with learning to read? Given the consistency of the evidence concerning reading volume and reading proficiency, the most useful initial discussions concern how much reading children should do during the school day.

How Much Reading do Children Need?

The answer to this question is fluid. This is because the necessary volume of reading seems to shift across developmental stages. In the initial stages, children cannot actually read very much—there is a limited supply of books they can manage successfully. And young children read much more slowly than older, more experienced readers. There is no agreed on metric for answering this question. Studies have calculated time spent reading, words read, pages read, and books read.

But what all these studies have consistently shown, regardless of how volume of reading was measured, was that there exists a potent relationship between volume of reading and reading achievement. The recent correlational data from the NAEP studies suggest that volume may be critically important in developing thoughtful literacy proficiencies. In addition, a variety of studies provide reliable, replicated evidence that children whose reading development lags behind their peers engage in far less reading than their higher-achieving peers. This has been found to be true even when these children participate in instructional support programs such as remedial reading or resource room.

It seems clear from these studies that the volume of daily in-school reading many children routinely experience is below an optimum level. So how much daily in-school reading might we plan for? I would suggest that one and one-half hours of daily in-school reading would seem a minimum goal given the data provided in the various studies. This would also seem to represent a substantial increase for many kids in most schools. In addition, ninety minutes of actual reading would still leave from four to four and one-half hours each day to accomplish other instructional activities. In other words, even ninety minutes of daily in-school reading would leave three-quarters of the school day (in a typical 6-hour day) available for other instructional activity.

Mind you that my ninety-minute recommendation is for time spent *actually reading*. Many schools allocate ninety minutes to reading instruction through grade 6. But much of that allocated time is not available for actual reading as other activities typically occupy large chunks of the allocated lesson time. In observing more and less effective elementary teachers (Allington & Johnston,

How More Effective Teachers Structure an Hour of Reading Lesson Time

The pattern of differences in reading (and writing) volume in more and less effective teachers' classrooms might be characterized by analyzing how one hour of time allocated to reading lessons might be used. In one of the schools where I observed, the more effective teacher routinely had children reading for forty to forty-five minutes of each hour allocated to reading instruction. She would spend five to ten minutes preparing the children to read the material and five to ten minutes engaging the children in activities following reading. While the children were reading the teacher worked with children, in small groups or individually side-by-side at their seats.

In the less effective teachers' classrooms the time allocated was the same but the time spent reading was typically quite different. These teachers often spent fifteen to twenty minutes preparing children to read, and twenty to twenty-five minutes after reading had the children engaged in a variety of follow-up activities, including responding to questions, completing workbook pages, reviewing the story, checking on vocabulary, and so on. Thus, in the less effective classrooms the children typically read for only fifteen to twenty minutes of each hour of time allocated to reading lessons and in some classrooms children read even less!

I observed similar disparities during social studies and science lessons, especially in the upper grades. The more effective teachers simply had students reading two and three times as much material in these content areas as did the less effective teachers.

2000; Pressley, et al., 2000; Taylor et al., 2000) sheer volume of reading was a distinguishing feature of the high-achievement classrooms.

Schools differ in how much time is allocated for reading and language arts instruction. Some set aside an hour and others set aside three hours each day. Even the various school reform models and instructional programs vary in the time recommended for reading and language arts instruction. One current high-visibility reading program suggests a two and one-half-hour daily reading instructional block. Another requires a daily minimum of ninety minutes of reading lessons with additional tutoring for children lagging behind. While both these programs are touted as successful "code-emphasis" programs, many folks seem to have not noticed that substantial allocations of instructional time for reading are at the core of both programs. Instead, these programs have been promoted as though there was some secret to success in the materials and methods these programs employ. However, virtually any reading intervention that reliably increases time engaged in reading should be expected to lead to achievement gains. In other words, what sometimes seems like evidence that a particular method or material produces higher achievement may actually be evidence that increasing reading volume positively affects reading achievement.

Time spent reading, my preferred measure of volume, is important. The research does not provide clear evidence on whether one type of reading is better than another. In other words, increasing the volume of oral or silent or choral or paired reading or almost any combination of these has been shown to enhance achievement. It does seem reasonable that older and more experienced readers might read more often silently and beginning readers might more often read aloud. But as long as children and adolescents are reading, the type of reading seems less critical.

Restructuring School Days to Make Time for Reading

In our work in schools—and our findings have been replicated by virtually every other research team conducting classroom-based research—we are typically distressed by how time in many schools and many classrooms is so very inefficiently organized. For instance, in many schools the official school day—the instructional day—begins at around 8:30 A.M. But at 8:30 A.M. in many schools, children are still on the playground or in the school cafeteria having just finished eating breakfast, when the bell rings signaling the beginning of the instructional day. At the bell, students begin the process of moving to their classrooms. This often involves lining up and waiting to be released to travel down the hall to enter the classroom. In some cases, students also have to stop off at lockers or cubbies to take off boots, hang up outerwear, and drop a backpack. After they enter the classroom, the teacher takes attendance, collects lunch money, book money, excuses for absences, homework, and other such administrative details. Then comes the Pledge of Allegiance and, often, morning announcements on the public address system. Finally, at 8:50 A.M., the teacher cues the children to take out their books and the instructional work actually begins. In these sorts of schools, students have already sat for twenty minutes of noninstructional activity—often more time than they will spend actually reading during the remainder of the day.

In some schools this sort of organizational inefficiency occurs not only at the beginning of the day but again at lunch and again at the end of the day. End-of-day routines often take another fifteen to twenty minutes—now more time has been spent on lining up, unpacking, packing up, and assorted other noninstructional activity than was spent reading and writing combined. In other words, for efficient use of scheduled instructional time teaching would continue until the very end of the official instructional day. If the instructional day ends at 2:30 P.M., then 2:30 is when kids should put down their books or journals and begin the management process of getting ready to go home. After 2:30 is when any afternoon announcement would be made over the public address system. But in too many schools where the instructional day ends at 2:30, the afternoon announcements and the getting-ready-to-go-home process begins at 2:15, not 2:30.

In many schools we can readily locate another thirty to fifty minutes every day for reading and writing activity. These are minutes that would be available if these schools were more efficiently organized. We must better organize schools to capture every minute of instructional time.

Capturing More Academic Time.   A good first step in planning for improved reading achievement is reworking the organization of the school day so that teachers and children have *all* of the official instructional time for productive academic work. This may mean rethinking procedures for taking attendance and getting needed information out. But some schools take attendance at break-fast, some have bus drivers do attendance reports, not teachers, and some have kids sign in when they arrive but before the school day begins. Book money, candy money, excuses for absence and all the other sorts of paperwork that waste instructional time can also be handled on a before-school basis by assign-ing paraprofessionals, clerks, or parent volunteers to stations where children bring the assorted paperwork. These stations can be in the breakfast area or entry area. Announcements can be posted on message boards to encourage children to apply their literacy skills.

The point here is that in most organizations it doesn't take fifteen to twenty minutes to begin work nor ten to fifteen minutes of the workday to get ready to go home. Imagine that you show up at a retail outlet that is scheduled to open at 8:30 but no one will open the doors until 8:50 because they are "get-ting ready" to work? Unfortunately, too many schools are organized this way. Even more unfortunate, in my experience, such organizational inefficiency is most common in lower-achieving schools.

To see just how instructionally efficient a school is, imagine walking the halls at the start of the school day and tallying how many children are reading or writ-ing (or doing math or science activities) within one minute of the official beginning of the instructional day. If the school day begins at 8:30, the goal should be hav-ing 100 percent of the children engaged in useful academic work at 8:31. Imagine walking the halls at the end of the official school day. How many classrooms have children working productively at 2:29 (assuming the day ends at 2:30). If your school, your classroom, uses many minutes of official instructional time for non-instructional activities (listening to morning announcements over the public address system is not instruction, neither is unpacking or packing up), you have located one area to begin your efforts for improving organizational efficiency.

Reading Lessons With Too Little Reading.   Sometimes we unintentionally cre-ate instructional plans that dramatically limit the volume of in-school reading. For instance, we routinely observe some teachers using whole class sets of a single tradebook within a three to six week (or more) unit. When we plan to spend six weeks on *Island of the Blue Dolphin*, we plan to limit children's read-ing and fill class time with other activities. Figure 2.2 provides the approximate reading times for several tradebooks that seem popular choices for extended unit. As a guide, 100 words per minute is an average silent reading rate for a second grader and 200 words per minute is about average for a fifth grader.

These numbers suggest that many teachers we have observed create plans that offer little reading volume, even in literature-based classrooms. And the sit-

Figure 2.2
Estimated Time Needed
to Read the Books
Listed at Different
Reading Rates (words
per minute=wpm)

Title	Approximate total words	200 words per minute	100 words per minute
Stone Fox (Gardiner)	12,000	2 hours	4 hours
Missing May (Rylant)	24,500	4 hours	8 hours
Hatchet (Paulsen)	50,000	8 hours	16 hours

uation is often exacerbated if the weekly lesson plan includes only a single literature excerpt from an anthology, as is too common in districts using a commercial reading series. The excerpts in most reading anthologies require no more twenty to thirty minutes to read. If the excerpt is the primary reading material in a week-long instructional unit, students will, by design, have limited opportunities to actually read.

A key problem with commercial reading series is that they often fill up vast amounts of lesson time with activities other than actual reading. Just consider that if an hour each day were allocated to reading lessons and the reading anthology excerpt only takes 30 minutes to read, then 270 minutes of lesson time each week must be filled with activities other than reading! Recall that engagement in reading has been found to be the most powerful instructional activity for fostering reading growth. Then why would publishers produce reading anthologies with but a single excerpted feature to read during a week-long reading lesson? Perhaps it is because with longer reading selections the anthologies would be, literally, too heavy for children to carry. Or perhaps purchasing a greater volume of literature would make the anthologies prohibitively expensive. Or maybe the traditional anthology is what most teachers want. Whatever the reason, the situation today is that no reading anthology contains enough reading material to develop high levels of reading proficiency in children.

In a number of the most effective classrooms I have observed, teachers used a commercial reading anthology but only one or two days per week. For instance, in one room this superbly effective teacher quickly introduced the basal selection to the children, assigned the story to be read in pairs, called the group back together about 30 minutes later to discuss the story and return to the text for a miniskill lesson. The students then were assigned a related page from the work text accompanying the series, which they completed, again, in pairs. That assignment was then discussed with the teacher the next morning before they began a new self-selected tradebook that would be their reading for the remainder of the week.

At the end of the school day I talked with the teacher about the pacing of the basal lesson. She said, "Dick, I just can't teach slow enough to make one of those stories last all week! I get bored and the kids get bored when we spend more than a day or so on one of the stories. If you have them in the right basal level, you don't need to teach and teach and teach all that stuff. I look through the teacher's manual and then just teach the few important things that my kids need."

It isn't just commercial reading series that offer too little reading volume. The same is true of the science and social studies textbooks as well. But, remember, the reading volume standards encompass all the reading children do during the school day so that enhancing the social studies curriculum with historical fiction, say, the Dear America series, or the science curriculum with Eyewitness books adds more volume for reading and more content knowledge as well.

Interruptions During the Day.   Another troublesome aspect of many school schedules is the number of interruptions that occur during the school day. There are three types of interruptions that are easily overlooked. The first has to do with interruptions of the classroom instructional day from special subject areas (e.g., music, art, physical education, computer lab, library, and so on). The second sort are the interruptions that occur when a few children leave to attend instructional support programs (e.g., resource room, speech, physical therapy, ESL lessons, remedial reading, psychological services, etc.). A common complaint among classroom teachers is that children come and go all day long making it difficult to plan and sustain comprehensive lessons. The third sort of interruption are those usually brief interruptions typified by public address announcements, brief queries at the classroom door from other teachers, counselors, specialists, paraprofessionals, parents, and other visitors. In some schools such interruptions commonly occur ten or more times each day. But these brief interruptions actually steal about three minutes each. That is the time that elapses from the point of interruption ("Jill, excuse me, but I'll need to see Jerome now.") through its end and until most children in the classroom are once again engaged in academic work. Now consider that ten such interruptions would eat up about thirty minutes of engaged instructional time. Every day. Two and one-half hours every week. Two whole school days every month!

Creating Uninterrupted Blocks for Instruction.   A good first principle in organizing a school more efficiently is to provide every classroom with at least two and one-half hours of uninterrupted time. No pull-outs, no push-ins, no specials. Then assure that other interruptions are minimized by eliminating use of the public address system during the instructional day except for true emergencies. Limit who can knock on a classroom door during the instructional day. Think about creating signs that say, *Teaching, Do Not Disturb,* and having them hang on classroom doorknobs. Some schools have limited student pick-up by parents to recess and lunch hour time periods as one way to reduce interruptions. This uninterrupted block does not have to be assigned exclusively to reading and language arts instruction (but doing so has some substantial benefits, especially when a more fully integrated curriculum is in place).

Creating the two-and-a-half-hour uninterrupted blocks begins by setting that as a firm organizational guideline. Currently, in too many schools, every special teacher creates a program that works best for them and classroom teachers have, literally, no control over this process. This sort of mindlessness has to end. Classroom teachers need time to teach. They need uninterrupted time to teach. Kids need time to learn. To read. To write. Uninterrupted learning time.

Rethinking the Design of Special Programs. It may be necessary to rethink special areas and support program designs. In some schools these programs now schedule fewer but longer periods of service to reduce the fragmentation of the instructional day. For instance, children receive special education services twice a week for fifty minutes rather than four times a week for twenty-five minutes. Art and music is scheduled every other week but for a double period (80 minutes instead of 40, for instance). These longer periods for special area subjects and support services can dramatically reduce the fragmentation observed in many classrooms. Reducing this fragmentation makes it easier for classroom teachers to design blocks of reading and writing time. It also makes it more likely that instructional time is lost to the interruptions and transitions that go with them.

In other cases, some special area classes and support services have moved outside the official school day. Instrumental music classes, remedial reading, speech, and resource services are offered before or after school for at least some kids. Reworking the work day for professional staff so that a flextime model is implemented allows schools to provide stronger and more comprehensive before- and after-school programs while also reducing the interruptions during the school day (Allington & Cunningham, 2001). In other words, classroom teachers might work with children on a traditional schedule of 8:30–2:30, while special area teachers and support teachers would work with children on a 10:30–4:30 schedule (or some variation of this).

One advantage of flextime is that schools can provide better services in after-school programs because with regular school staff providing the services, there are greater opportunities for coordinating lessons with those of classroom curriculum. In addition, core curriculum instructional time increases as some of the support instruction is moved outside the traditional day. This seems especially useful for lower-achieving children. No longer do they miss some of the classroom instruction while participating in speech and language training, remedial reading, or physical therapy. Such use of flextime also allows schools to offer richer after-school programs without so much added expense.

Unfortunately, teachers often have little say in such matters. Nonetheless, classroom and specialist teachers, even individually, need to begin to request the sorts of shifts discussed above. However, such requests seem more effective when they come from a team or a set of grade-level teachers. For instance, in one school the fourth- and fifth-grade teachers requested a restructuring of the various special services their children received. The problem was that children seemed constantly coming and going. It was difficult to keep track of who had missed what. Ultimately, a new schedule was created that had every fourth and fifth-grade classroom receiving two sixty to ninety minute blocks of consultant support each week. Writing workshops were scheduled during these periods and the remedial and resource teachers worked in the rooms as coteachers though they emphasized instructional support for the students that were eligible for instructional support. In the end, the support services were better coordinated with the classroom curriculum and the instruction better linked to state standards as required by federal law. The classroom teachers not only had fewer interruptions but a second set of expert hands to provide needed instruction. The students now completed more writing and benefited from the reduction in daily lesson fragmentation.

Creating Standards for Reading Volume in the Elementary Grades.   Schools should develop an agreed on standard for expected volume of reading (and writing). When school has no such standard, wide variation from classroom to classroom seems to be the norm. When creating reading volume standards, plan on using all sorts of reading in developing the standards. That is, reading in science, social studies, or other content areas should be counted in calculating the volume standards. Guided reading, self-selected reading, partner reading, buddy reading, and every other sort of actual reading would be considered in estimating school-day reading volume. Once a professional staff agrees on such standards, it should not be surprising that the variation in how much students read during the school day is substantially reduced. It should not be surprising to find that students actually read more as well.

Along with my ninety-minute volume standard for daily in-school reading, I would also set a thirty- to forty-five-minute volume standard for writing. Thus, about two hours of the instructional day would be allocated to just reading or writing (including reading and writing in content subjects also). The reciprocal relationship between reading and writing opportunities and proficiencies has been well established (Tierney & Shanahan, 1984), particularly the links between comprehension and composing.

Volume standards could also be developed for a week rather than a day. The advantage with such a scheme is the greater flexibility in creating lesson plans. For instance, using weekly volume standards (comparable to summing my daily standards) would allow for a full half-day allocation (150 minutes) for writing activity with time left over for shorter (10–15 minutes) daily writing opportunities. In some classrooms, especially at the upper grades, use of such longer blocks of time can be especially useful when students are working on thematic reports, projects, or simply taking a longer piece of writing to the publish stage. The use of fewer but longer blocks of time for reading should also be considered. Imagine a fourth-grade student being able to complete a whole book during a single day? The way an adult might read a book—in a single setting.

If one day was essentially set aside for reading opportunity and a half-day was set aside for writing activity we could still have time for an hour of reading on three remaining days and an hour of writing on one other day and still have used only 40 percent of the instructional time for the week. If the read-

---

Whole-Day Plan

One "thinking outside the box" activity that schools might consider is Dr. Dick's Whole-Day Plan (WDP). The WDP involves scheduling just one subject a day. Thus, Monday is Social Studies Day, Tuesday is Reading Day, Wednesday is Math Day, Thursday is Writing Day, and Friday is Science Day. Kids do Science all day on Friday—that's right, *all day*. They do the other subjects all day on the other days. This activity literally forces us to rethink the chopped-up school day. It forces us to rethink lesson planning. It creates wonderful opportunities for extended reading and writing and for research and project work and so on. It isn't the case that the WDP would necessarily continue all year. Maybe only a week. But, in my experience, even a week teaching in the WDP creates an enthusiasm for the possibilities of fewer, longer curriculum blocks during the school week.

---

ing and writing were sometimes related to science or social studies, we could probably expand the reading and writing blocks even more.

Longer blocks of time for reading and writing seem a more authentic instructional plan in the sense that to get truly involved in a book usually requires something more than a ten-minute block of time. Langer's work (1995) suggests that it takes a while to "get lost in a book." But getting lost in a book is the essence of skilled reading. I have helped schools organize whole-day reading and whole-day writing days—where everyone read or wrote all day long. Both students and teachers reported some amazing responses to these experiments in lots of reading and writing time. The most common response was positive and along the lines of, "It was so cool to be able to finish the whole book." Or, "I love being able to really work, like all day, on my report." Think of how you write when a report is due for a graduate class. Think about how you read when you finally sit down with the latest novel from your favorite author.

I am not suggesting that every day be a just reading or just writing day. My point is that far too much school reading and writing is marked by brief periods of reading or writing activity followed by an interruption—usually in the middle of a paragraph—and then a shift in activity. Our schools demand lots of low-level, short-reading activities (e.g., a section of a social studies chapter, ten minutes of DEAR, a paragraph on a social studies worksheet) and lots of brief, shallow writing activities (e.g., three minutes to write in a daily journal, 10 minutes to write responses to end-of-chapter questions, 15 minutes to compose a short persuasive essay). But in the world outside of school people read at least whole chapters and whole articles at one sitting. They write complete letters to the editor, persuasive essays, shopping lists, and reports as a single episode, not as a series of five- to ten-minute activities. It takes time to read deeply and to write thoughtfully. But in school, too often, "reading/writing interruptus" is the working model of lesson design. Such a design may be more effective in undermining real reading and writing activity than we could imagine, especially for children who don't read much outside of school.

Reading and Writing Volume in the Grades 6–12.   Given the reported decline in volume of reading and writing that begins at the middle-school level and the slow growth of reading proficiency in grades 5–12 (NCES), planning for reading and writing volume must be a K–12 concern. It seems odd that as students' reading and writing proficiency improves, schools expect less reading and less writing in and out of school. The NAEP survey data illustrates this pattern quite well.

After a period of experimentation in the 1970s and 1980s, with a larger role for tradebooks in content area classes, especially in the social studies and the English language arts, most middle school and high school content classes have returned to using a single textbook as the primary curriculum source. Even literature courses often emphasize the use of an anthology of short stories and excerpts from novels and other longer works (Applebee, 1991).

The single-source—usually a textbook—curriculum plan has a number of limitations if student learning is the focus. One primary difficulty is that the reliance on a single textbook dramatically limits the amount of reading students do in the course. The minimal reading and writing requirements of most high school courses was first driven home when I sat, as a parent, at a high school-sponsored "getting ready for college" session that featured commentary from several college students. What struck me was their assertion that one of the greatest differences between college and high school was the sheer volume of reading and writing that was expected in college compared to what had been required in high school.

As one of the college students noted, and the others vigorously agreed, "Almost any one of my professors requires more reading and writing for a single course than was required by all of my high school teachers together during my senior year." As these college students then went on to discuss courses with weekly writing assignments, with three textbooks or eight tradebooks as the curriculum sources, with research papers in abundance, I quickly thought back across the senior year one of my kids had just finished. Even with a couple of AP courses, there was little reading or writing expected.

Failure to keep up with college reading and writing demands seems to be a primary difficulty for even the best of our high school students, those admitted to four-year colleges. But with the very modest volume of reading and writing in high school, it is not, perhaps, surprising that fewer than half of all entering college students complete a degree within six years.

But lots more reading in grades 6–12 isn't just needed to better prepare students for college. When adolescents read more they broaden and deepen their content knowledge as well. High school students who have only read their American history textbooks are not likely to know much about American history. In the same sense, students who have read beyond their biology textbooks know more about biology—and about thinking like a biologist—than purely textbook-bound students.

American textbooks used in grades K–12 have been described as offering a curriculum plan that is "a mile wide and an inch deep." In other words, most school textbooks are designed to foster a very limited understanding of a wide range of topics. Researchers have also demonstrated that most textbooks are "inconsiderate" texts because they are so rarely well written. Yet the use of a textbook as the sole curriculum resource dominates middle- and high school classrooms.

USA Today (September 29, 1999), in a front-page article titled, *Failing Grades for Science Books*, noted that a study conducted by the Association for the Advancement of Science had concluded that "those thick, heavy science textbooks middle school students lug around are full of disconnected facts and irrelevant classroom activities." The study also reported that the texts (1) covered too many topics, (2) failed to develop any topic well, and (3) offered classroom activities that were nearly useless in fostering understanding of key concepts. The authors of the report concluded that the textbooks "neither educate or motivate" students.

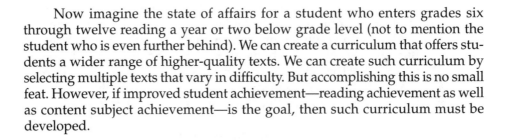

Now imagine the state of affairs for a student who enters grades six through twelve reading a year or two below grade level (not to mention the student who is even further behind). We can create a curriculum that offers students a wider range of higher-quality texts. We can create such curriculum by selecting multiple texts that vary in difficulty. But accomplishing this is no small feat. However, if improved student achievement—reading achievement as well as content subject achievement—is the goal, then such curriculum must be developed.

SUMMARY

Kids need to read a lot if they are to become good readers. The evidence on this point is overwhelming. To ensure that all students read a lot, schools need to develop standards for expected volume of reading (and writing). The cornerstone of an effective school organizational plan is allocating sufficient time for lots of reading and writing. Some of the time needed can be reclaimed from non-instructional activities. But it is important that such a plan has the support of teachers. All teachers must understand the enormous benefits that enhancing the volume of reading will provide. In such a plan there would be long blocks of uninterrupted time for reading and writing. Reading and writing would be integrated across all subject areas and a curriculum that featured wide reading and writing of informational texts as well as narratives would frame the lessons and activities. The plan would encompass grades K–12, not just the elementary grades.

3

KIDS NEED BOOKS
THEY CAN READ

Before they leave on vacation, few adults wander down to their nearest university library looking for thick, hard books on topics they don't care about. In fact, adults generally, including college-educated adults, avoid hard reading whenever possible. This accounts for the popularity of magazines that offer writing that is rated as high school-level difficulty. If folks liked hard reading, then magazines such as *Scientific American* or *The Economist* would out-sell *Newsweek* and *People*. But they don't.

All readers generally prefer reading that is less demanding—unless their interest in a topic is incredibly high. Only then will most readers tolerate hard reading. I don't think kids are very much different from adults in this regard. But adults seem always to prefer that children read difficult books rather than easy books. The evidence available has convinced me that lots of easy reading is absolutely critical to reading development and to the development of positive stances toward reading. So why is assigning easy reading so often ignored in schools? In this chapter we will explore that question and examine the research on easy reading and matching kids with "just right" books.

TASK DIFFICULTY AND ACHIEVEMENT

The issue of the difficulty of schoolwork was widely studied in the 1970s and 1980s. Researchers investigated the relationship between task difficulty and achievement gains in elementary school classrooms in an attempt to better understand effective teaching. One of the largest such studies was the Beginning Teacher Evaluation Study (Denham & Lieberman, 1980). In the BTES study, three student success rates were defined: *high*, meaning students worked at tasks that were very easy; *moderate*, when students exhibited partial mastery but the tasks were somewhat easy; and *low*, for tasks that the students found hard and in which they made many errors. The researchers (Berliner, 1981) found that success rates had a substantial impact on student learning. They produced strong, consistent evidence that tasks completed with high rates of success were linked to greater learning and improved student attitudes toward the subject matter being learned, while tasks where students were moderately successful were less consistently related to learning and hard tasks produced a negative impact on learning. Hard tasks also produced off-task behaviors and negative attitudes. That is, students given tasks where success was low were far more likely to cease work on the task and engage in nonacademic behaviors than were students working at high success rates.

Thus, many classroom management difficulties were linked to the relative difficulty of school work students were given. The fact that success rate could be manipulated was also seen as important because it suggested that when schools wanted to improve student achievement, success rate could be enhanced by redesigning lessons. When lessons were redesigned so that success was more widespread, student engagement rates improved as did their learning.

Gambrell, Wilson, and Gannt (1981) indicated that oral reading error rates of 5 percent or greater were linked to significant increases in off-task behavior largely replicating the findings of the BTES researchers. But Betts (1946) deserves the credit for drawing attention to the issue of success rate while reading. He studied fourth-grade students and reported that relatively low error rates seemed to produce improved learning. He established criteria for three levels of difficulty. His *independent*-level reading was marked by high word-recognition accuracy (98% or better), fluent reading (phrases with intonation), and strong comprehension of the material read (90% comprehension accuracy). Texts at this level of difficulty were viewed as appropriate for the reading children did with no assistance and little, if any, instruction from adults. His *instructional*-level criteria—for material used in lessons where the teacher provided instruction on

---

Quick Check for Appropriateness of Reading Materials

There is a quick way to get a quick sense of the appropriateness of the reading materials different children in your classroom have available. First, select six children—two each from high, middle, and lower achievers. Second, make an hour or so available (or two ½-hour periods) and sit for 10 minutes with each child at his or her desk. Third, as you do this, have each child read aloud 100 words from every book in his or her desk, including science and social studies books. As the students read, rate their fluency as good, fair, or poor based on the guidelines provided below. Finally, note the number of books that students read with a *Poor* fluency rating. This will give you a quick estimate as to whether many kids seem to have inappropriate books available—that is, books with which they can be expected to experience limited success.

Good—Reads in phrases, with intonation.
Fair—Reads in phrases mostly, often lacks appropriate intonation.
Poor—Reads mostly word-by-word.

the material and reading support—also required relatively high accuracy (95–97%), phrase reading, and good comprehension (75%). Betts argued that *frustration*-level reading—accuracy below 95 percent, word-by-word reading, and comprehension below 75 percent—was to be avoided because of the negative impact such experiences had on both learning and attitude.

The importance of accuracy in reading texts has been demonstrated in several other studies. Juel's (1994) longitudinal study indicated that "quality of word recognition in first grade (i.e., being able to recognize words) is more important than quantity of exposure to words... but once there is high quality word recognition... quantity of reading becomes critical" (p. 124). Likewise, Swanson and Hoskyn's (1998) meta-analysis of 180 intervention studies with learning disabled students identified only three factors that contributed unique variance to achievement. Control of task difficulty was one of those three factors. When students were given tasks that were difficult, achievement gains were hard to come by.

But in some schools students seem routinely placed in texts that are too difficult if optimum achievement is the goal. Consider that Chall and Conard (1991) found that only one of the eighteen elementary science and social studies books they examined had readability levels at the grade level of intended use. While most of these books were one or two grade levels above the designated grade level for use, the difficulty of four of the textbooks were three to four grade levels above the grade in which they were commonly used. As for the reading anthologies, they found that between 40 and 60 percent of the elementary students of average achievement levels were working with reading texts considered appropriate given their reading achievement on standardized tests—the rest, almost half of the average students—were using materials considered too difficult. The case was substantially worse for lower-achieving students.

When Chall and Conard (1991) assessed elementary students' comprehension of their textbooks directly, somewhere between one-quarter and one-half of the average-achievement elementary students achieved a satisfactory comprehension performance of their science and social studies books while none of the lower-achieving students met the comprehension criteria after reading those books. (Their analysis of middle-school and high school textbooks indicated that these were more often written at levels comparable to the grade levels in which they were used and were sometimes rated as below the grade level of use.) All this suggests that many, many elementary students are confronted daily by texts that are too complex for optimum learning.

Thus, for over fifty years the use of Betts's criteria has been recommended in an attempt to match students with texts that would optimize learning. But too often, over this same period, teachers have been mandated to place all children in the same texts, regardless of the match between the child's level of reading development and the complexity of the texts in the mandated curriculum. And when not mandated to do so, teachers often had few options, as schools supplied multiple copies of only a single social studies text, for instance, intended for use by all students. But since Betts's (1946) original study, the evidence has accumulated supporting his position (Allington, 1984). Having said that, let me note that I think any set of specific criteria need to be used somewhat flexibly. But flexibility is not a characteristic of the "one-size-fits-all" reforms that are appearing in school after school.

The key point here is that the research has well demonstrated the need for students to have instructional texts that they can read accurately, fluently, and with good comprehension if we hope to foster academic achievement. The evidence also suggests that for large numbers of students this recommendation has been routinely ignored. But if we are to address the issue more satisfactorily, what methods can be used to determine whether the texts available for instruction are of an appropriate level of difficulty?

"Historically, public schools in the United States have been built on the assumption that not every student can learn well and, hence, many students must make learning errors…. Accordingly, schools were designed to allow these many error-full learners to distinguish themselves from their few error-free peers. Most students rather than being given chance after chance in our public schools to demonstrate learning success, were given chance after chance to demonstrate learning mediocrity or failure…. If we want to produce a generation of truly learned students, then the learning student cannot experience success at only a few milestones in his/her career. Each must experience a *constant* stream of success [emphasis added]."

(Block, 1980, pp. 98–99)

METHODS FOR ESTIMATING TEXT COMPLEXITY

The most common approach to estimating the difficulty of texts has been the use of structural readability formulas. There are a variety of such formulas available but each of the formulas rely primarily on two structural measures of text difficulty: word difficulty (estimated the frequency of use or word length) and sentence complexity (most often measured by sentence length). But the estimates of text difficulty from any of these procedures is just that—an estimate. All formulas have some error in measurement and all suffer from one problem. That problem is that both of the sentences below would be rated at the same level of difficulty!

John went to the store. He bought some candy.
Candy some bought he. Store the to went John.

Structural readability formulas cannot tell whether text is well written or even whether it makes sense. Similarly, these formulas cannot examine picture support, interestingness, or a student's prior knowledge about the topic being presented. And yet each of these factors have been shown to influence the difficulty of texts for students (Klare, 1984). Thus, use of any of the readability formulas provides, at best, a very crude estimate of the difficulty students might have with a text.

Some would argue that such weaknesses are good reason to avoid calculating readability estimates from the structural formulas. My view, however, is that the use of such formulas can be useful if only for providing a ballpark estimate of text difficulty. Even a ballpark estimate is better than none at all.

Several of the structural readability procedures are currently in fairly widespread use and discussed below.

The *Dale-Chall Readability Formula* (Chall & Dale, 1995) has been around for fifty years, although it was recently updated. It works best on upper-elementary materials and above and provides a two-year difficulty band estimate (grades 5–6 difficulty), which nicely emphasizes the notion of an "estimated" level of difficulty. The procedure is available on the *Readability Master 2000* software (1-800-666-BOOK), and when this process is used, one only has to type in samples of text and the calculations are completed automatically.

The *Flesch-Kincaid Formula* has also been available for fifty years and was revised in the 1970s. Microsoft Word word processing software incorporates this formula for estimating the difficulty of documents. (Go to the Grammar feature under Preferences and click on Document Statistics.) Again, by typing in text samples (or scanning them in) we can get an estimate, in grade level terms, of the difficulty.

The *Degrees of Reading Power* (DRP) procedure (Koslin, Zeno & Koslin, 1987) provides estimates of text difficulty on a unique scale that is linked directly to achievement levels on the DRP standardized reading achievement test. The developers suggest that using the scores on the DRP test and the DRP estimates of text difficulty provides a more reliable match between texts and students compared to the traditional procedure of using a standard readability formula estimate and a standardized test score to attempt to match kids and books. The support for this argument centers on the integration of the DRP measurement technique into both the formula and the test item development. The publishers, Touchstone Applied Science (www.tasaliteracy.com) also offer computer software with over 12,500 textbooks and tradebooks rated by difficulty. This software allows searches for texts on particular topics within a specified difficulty range. They also provide a conversion table for converting DRP difficulty levels into grade-level equivalents (although they prefer that schools use the DRP assessment and difficulty ratings in tandem). Advantage Learning now uses the DRP readability with its Accelerated Reader program.

The *Lexile Framework* (Stenner, 1996) shares many features with the DRP in that it provides difficulty estimates on a unique scale (although, again, conversion to grade-level equivalents is possible though not recommended). However, the procedure for estimating text difficulty is different and more similar to the procedure used in the Dale-Chall formula. The developers of the Lexile Framework, however, have negotiated agreements with some publishers of texts and tradebooks and publishers of achievement tests so that they might offer services for matching kids and books much like the DRP developers. Currently, the Scholastic *Reading Counts* (www.readingcounts.com) system offers access to 25,000 titles rated for difficulty on several formulas (e.g., Lexile, DRP). The system includes a Book Expert search option that allows you to locate books on topics within a specified difficulty range. Another neat feature is the book awards option. Schools can purchase twelve books for $12.00 to use as incentives for completing a specified amount of reading. These books come with a special gold seal indicating the award.

Advantage Learning Systems, developers of the *Accelerated Reader* seems currently the most widely used commercial system for matching students with books (Institute for Academic Excellence, 1998). They also offer *STAR Reading,* a computer-adaptive reading test that promises to estimate a student's reading achievement and then provide lists of book titles that would be good fits with the student's level of reading development. They also publish tables that allow teachers to correlate any standardized achievement test score to book difficulty levels. Finally, the Accelerated Reader BookGuide software (1-800-831-4190) is designed to provide an easy search of 22,000 tradebook titles as well as features. However, the past dominance of this system is being challenged by new entries into the marketplace.

Book Adventure is a new web-based management tool developed by Sylvan Learning Foundation in partnership with Barnes & Noble, Houghton-Mifflin, Canter, Bowker, and Lycos. A primary advantage is that the tool is offered at no charge. The Book Adventure website provides approximately 10,000 books to choose from. These titles are organized into approximately 40 interest categories. Students can search by interest, grade level difficulty, author, and title or they can use an automated "Help me find a book" search which creates potential book lists at specified levels of difficulty within the three interest categories specified. However, the difficulty rating of the books was assigned by the book's publisher and included in Children's Books in Print. The difficulty levels are often expressed as a grade level range (e.g., grades 2–5, 5–12) and seem to suggest interest level as much as difficulty level. The end-of-book quizzes are individually generated from an item bank so no two quizzes are necessarily like.

But this product supplies no book collections. Instead, books that students identify can be requested from the school or public library or there is an option of linking to the Barnes & Noble website to order individual books directly. Of course, this means that someone has to have a credit card to have established an account with Barnes & Noble to have this feature work.

None of the technology tools seem to have adequate research to support claims of improved student achievement. The tools, however, do seem to offer different advantages. The web-based *Reading Adventure* tool allows searches from virtually any computer and eliminates the "messiness" of CD-ROM software. However, the system currently lists half as many titles as *Accelerated Reader* and *Reading Counts!* In addition, the assignment of text difficulty levels in *Reading Adventure* is crude in comparison to the other products' use of the more sophisticated Lexile and DRP frameworks.

So which method is preferred? My response is, it depends. I prefer the methods that allow teachers to estimate text difficulty in grade levels, since that metric is commonly understood (although hardly precise). These are also the least expensive methods since you simply purchase a copy of the readability disk or word processing software and go about calculating estimated difficulty levels in grade equivalents. But this method is time consuming if there are large numbers of books to be rated. In such cases, using the DRP or Lexile materials, each which have the difficulty of thousands of books already estimated, seems more sensible. However, the computer-based systems work best when linked to the developers' assessment materials and that will drive the costs substantially while not necessarily improving the accuracy of the estimates.

The *Accelerated Reader* and the *Reading Counts!* programs provide the computerized testing, a large supply of books rated for difficulty, and even a reading monitoring system (e.g., quizzes). But these can be expensive options and there is no instructional support, per se. The monitoring systems, unfortunately, seem dated and offer primarily low-level recall questions for students to answer after completing each chapter. Much of what we know about the power of high-quality comprehension strategy instruction and the potential of group discussion in fostering students' understanding is omitted from the design of these programs. But these packages might be useful in schools where teachers are largely unfamiliar with children's books and where paraprofessionals are available to manage the program, while teachers offer the expert reading instruction as well as opportunities for student discussion that are missing in the commercial package.

These various options for estimating text difficulty, in the hopes of better matching children with appropriate reading materials, all have a potential role in making it more likely that children will have access to books they can actually read and learn to read with. But, as noted earlier, all such procedures have inherent problems and the estimates are best considered ballpark estimates than an estimate with any sort of scientific specificity. When teachers know their students well and are more expert about estimating the complexity of texts, they often do not need readability estimates to find appropriate books for the children in their classrooms.

Leveling Books

Marie Clay, the developer of the *Reading Recovery* intervention that has demonstrated such high levels of success in accelerating the reading development of first graders in trouble, deserves much credit for refocusing our attention on the importance of matching children with books at an appropriate level of complexity. In the *Reading Recovery* program a central tenet involves moving the child successfully through a sequence of increasingly difficult little books. Now, gradually increasing the complexity of the difficulty of school texts is not a new idea by any means. But, historically, such gradations were rather crude. There were, for instance, five levels of complexity in the traditional basal series across first and second grade (preprimer, primer, first reader, first second reader, second second reader). But *Reading Recovery* sliced this into twenty four levels of complexity.

The development of these levels followed a different sort of procedure than that followed traditionally by publishers. Instead of calculating difficulty levels from structural readability formulas, Clay, and her colleagues in New

Zealand and the United States, actually tried the books out with children! They recorded the difficulty children had and used that information to locate each book within a level of difficulty. In addition, they examined a variety of text features ignored in structural readability formulas. They examined illustrations and their supportiveness; layout of the book; and text structures such as repetition of language, predictability of the story line, and the familiarity of the context and content.

More recently, Fountas and Pinnell (1999) have extended this line of work, with some modifications, including extending the leveling process through fourth-grade material and reducing the number of levels by about half. Their text, *Matching Books to Readers* (Heinemann, www.heinemann.com) provides the difficulty levels of over 7,500 titles that have been widely used with children across grades K – 4.

In addition, many publishers now provide book levels for their books but there is no agreed on framework for the levels reported. Some publishers use a numbering system (e.g., levels 1, 2, 3,...) that looks similar to the *Reading Recovery* levels but the similarity is typically misleading in that the two sets of numbers have no real demonstrated relationship to one another. Other publishers use an alphabetic system (e.g., levels A, B, C,...) that appears similar to the Fountas and Pinnell (1999) levels but, again, are not equivalent.

Thus, teachers are left with a not insignificant problem. Lots of texts leveled through lots of different processes. What is a teacher to do?

Leveling your books.   In our work with teachers and their school districts, we have found that the problem of leveling books is less a problem than it seems. We have used an adaptation of the procedure recommended in Chall and her colleagues (1996). Her book offers a "qualitative assessment" of book difficulty. Basically, the leveling process involves the use of "benchmark texts"—texts that represent different grade levels or segments of a grade level (beginning-second-, middle-second, and late-second-grade texts). The Chall et al. (1996) worktext provides such benchmark texts, but drawing on a handful of books at any level from the Fountas and Pinnell (1999) listing seems to work just as well. Once you have the benchmark books at hand, the procedure is as follows:

1. Take the book to be leveled and skim through it, looking at the page format, type size, sentence length, topic familiarity, vocabulary familiarity, and story predictability.
2. Now look at the benchmark books. Find the benchmark book that most closely approximates the difficulty of the book to be leveled. Once located, label the new book the same level as the benchmark book. Now as the year progresses, ask yourself, Do kids who can read the benchmark book successfully also seem successful in the newly labeled book? If so, then let the level stand. If not, relabel the book as a level or so harder (or easier if students seem to have significantly less difficulty with it).

Involving groups of teachers in the book-leveling process—primary in one group, intermediate grade teachers in another—seems to result in two positive benefits. First, the levels are more reliable when several sets of eyes make the leveling judgment. And there are more kids reading the books who provide more teachers with more feedback on the reliability of the leveling. Second, as teachers go through the leveling process they develop greater expertise in estimating book difficulty. As they monitor book difficulty across the year, they develop an enhanced sensitivity to the book-kid matching problem. (McGill-Franzen, 1993)

Teach Kids the Three-Finger Rule.   An astonishingly simple strategy that needs to be added to every classroom is the three-finger rule. Just tell kids to read the first page or two of the book (depending on the number of words on a page) and to hold up a finger for every word they cannot read. If they get to three fingers up, the book is probably too hard and they should look for another one (unless the topic is near and dear to them). Now this is hardly scientific but it is a tried and tested classroom method. I think the key understanding being developed here is one that is important for kids to develop. That is, some books are just too hard. I would point out that there are books adults find too hard. Tax manuals, for instance. So they pay someone else to read them and figure things out. But learning that selecting appropriate books is important is an important understanding itself.

Observe Kids Reading to Better Match Them with Books.   In the end, no matter what procedure is used to attempt to put more appropriate books into the hands of students, it comes down to each kid and each book. Every procedure discussed thus far provides an *estimate* of the fit between a kid and a book. And estimates are always just estimates. Estimates help us find books that seem good choices given a child's level of development. But estimates are not always good enough.

Once a child has a book in his or her hands, we can observe whether the book seems to "fit" the child. There are both far observations and near observations that can help us determine the fit of the book.

Far Observations. Look around the classroom during a silent reading period. Are there children whose bodies, faces, or even fingers provide signs of frustration? Are there kids who seem to be "wandering"—mentally or physically—when they should be reading? Do some kids have the book close to their face, brow furrowed, and finger-stabbing at the words? Do some kids turn the page much less often than others—or at all? If this is a grade 3–6 classroom, can you hear subvocalizing? Observe much lip movement and finger following of the text?

All of the above could be considered possible indicators that children are reading only with difficulty. Now, be cautious, however, because almost any of these indicators can also represent something else going badly that day. But frustration-level reading activity is, well, frustrating, and you can often observe that frustration from afar and well before it breaks through the surface and produces a "discipline event."

Near Observations. Now move up close to, alongside actually, children who seem to be experiencing difficulty. Many times they are subvocalizing and you need only to sit there to hear the difficulty they are having. At other times you might want to have them read a bit softly to you. Perhaps they can read aloud a passage they just completed as you arrived (especially if they seem to be struggling—if they still struggle after having already read it they are in a text that is truly too hard). As they read to you, you need to be taking notes.

Record the Accuracy of the Word Recognition.   The simplest procedure for this is simply a modification of the "running records" strategy developed by Clay (1993). Have a spiral notebook along. Write the page number of the book at the top of the page (and maybe the book title). Now as the child reads, simply jot a check mark for every word correctly pronounced and an X for each word mispronounced. Put checks and X's in rows that match the text being read. That is, every time the child reads a new line, drop down and begin a new row of checks and X's. Also note the fluency level: *Good, Fair, Poor.* After a few pages thank the child and move away and calculate the overall accuracy (number of words read correctly divided by total words in the passage) and fluency rates and write them at the bottom of the page and circle them. Note also whether this was a first reading or a repeated reading of the text. Note that these procedures are not meant to be a formal diagnosis. The purpose is primarily to assess the appropriateness of the text the student is reading in an up-close manner. The process should be completed rather quickly because the goal is a better estimate of the text's appropriateness than is provided by the readability estimates or the book's estimated level. Remember, we want children to have consistently successful experiences with the texts they read. Regular monitoring of the difficulty, or lack of it, that students experience is a necessary component of effective instruction.

A Completed Accuracy Record

Ideally, children would be reading with a high level of accuracy (95+ percent correct words) and at least a *fair* level of fluency. Such are the typical characteristics of readers reading appropriate books. These are the books that allow children and adolescents to develop and polish useful reading strategies.

Text child read aloud:	*Teacher's record:*
tried	
Minny was ~~tired~~ of walking.	✔ ✔ X ✔ ✔
She just wanted to sit down and rest.	✔ ✔ ✔ ✔ ✔ ✔ ✔ ✔
But, there were so many people at the fair	✔ ✔ ✔ ✔ ✔ ✔ ✔ ✔ ✔
that there seemed to be no place to sit.	✔ ✔ ✔ ✔ ✔ ✔ ✔ ✔

When 30/31 words are read acurately = 97% accuracy.

Recall Summary

Finding out about how well the text is understood is also important. The most direct method for such an assessment is to ask the child to retell what has been read. Just listen at first and, perhaps, prompt with, "Can you tell me more?" Teachers can make quite good judgments about children's understandings of texts using this simple, time honored method of evaluating understanding. Because continuing to read makes little sense if there is no understanding, every near observation should entail some assessment of how well the material is being understood. After the retelling, complete the recall summary shown below.

After the child provides an oral summary of the text simply place a check next to each text element included in the summary.

For narratives:

Key characters? _____
Setting? _____
Story line? _____
Story ending? _____

For informational texts:

Key topic? _____
Major facts? _____
Link to prior knowledge? _____

ENHANCING ACCESS TO APPROPRIATE BOOKS

There are certain sorts of classroom environments that make teaching not only easier but more productive. One key feature is a large supply of books across a range of difficulty levels—a range at least as wide as the range of reading achievement levels of the students who come to that room every day. The classrooms of our exemplary teachers (Pressley et al. 2000) invariably had a much larger supply of books than were found in the typical classrooms in the school they worked in. In our earlier work (Allington et al., 1996; Guice et al., 1997; Johnston et al., 1998) we had noted that:

- higher achieving schools had more books in classroom library collections than were found in lower-achieving schools;
- schools in wealthier neighborhoods had classrooms with larger book collections than were found in schools in poorer neighborhoods;
- classrooms with a larger supply of books had kids who read more frequently;
- classrooms with a larger supply of books usually had more kids reading books they could manage successfully.

These findings replicated the findings from other studies (e.g., Dickinson & Smith, 1998; Knapp, 1995; Morrow, 1992; Robinson, Larsen & Haupt, 1996; Smith, Constantino & Krashen, 1997) demonstrating the potential of easy access to a wide range of books of appropriate complexity on children's reading opportunities and, ultimately, on achievement.

In this school the custodian installed plastic rain gutters below the chalk trays so that many books could be displayed with the covers showing.

The classrooms that were best able to put appropriate books into kids' hands (and into their desks), had hundreds of titles available in the classroom collection. These titles represented a substantial range of difficulty as well as a range of genres. In other words, these hundreds of books were not, typically, class sets of a few titles (25 copies of 10 children's books). While there were, in some rooms, class sets of particular titles, we more often found smaller sets, say five copies, of some titles with the quantity of books accounted for primarily by single copies of many, many books. If I were required to establish guidelines for quantity, I would recommend at least 500 different books in every classroom with those split about evenly between narratives and informational books and about equally between books that are on or near grade-level difficulty and books that are below grade level.

As with all criteria, no specific quantity can serve all classrooms equally well. For instance, beginning readers can, and should, read multiple books every day. In the exemplary first-grade classrooms we studied it was common for children to read 10 or more titles every day (counting rereading of books). Thus, 500 titles do not go as far in first grade as they do in a fifth-grade classroom where children might be expected to read a title a week. But by fifth grade, there is often both a wider range of achievement and a wider array of books than might be included in a first grade collection. (I should also note that many of the exemplary teachers we studied had classroom collections in the 1,500 book titles range.)

Two other factors influence the numbers of books needed in a classroom collection: Ease of access to books in the school library and the availability of supplies of books for use in the classroom.

School Libraries Stacked with Outdated Volumes

"Man has not landed on the moon. The Soviet Union still exists. African-Americans are negroes. Proper ladies wear hats and never compete with men. Penicillin is a new discovery. Welcome to the world of the public school library and The Book Shelves Time Forgot." Thus read the headline and introduction in an article that appeared in the *Boston Globe* (January 18, 2000). The article noted that the typical Boston public school elementary library contained 1,000–2,000 volumes but with half or more of those books woefully outdated. The article didn't note that such a collection is 10,000 or more books short of the American Library Association's standard for a small elementary school. Unfortunately, the Boston school libraries reflect what seems to be a common deficiency in urban schools—far too few books and those available are often racist, sexist, and outdated. The most outrageously inappropriate book mentioned in the *Globe* article was one titled "A young woman's guide to business" that contained a cartoon illustration of a young woman being chased around a desk by an older male!

Ease of Access to Books in the School Library.   School libraries vary enormously in the size and adequacy of their collections, the availability, supportiveness, and expertise of the library staff, and the actual access children have to the library and its books (Krashen, 1993; McQuillan, 1998). But adequately stocked and staffed school libraries are essential, even when classroom collections number into the hundreds of books. School libraries will always have resources that are unavailable in the classroom (or at least well-stocked school libraries will). The library will have a deeper and broader collection of texts (and other information resources) than can be supplied to any given classroom. Unfortunately, school library resources are directly linked to community wealth. That is, a consistent finding in study after study is that schools that enroll many children from low-income families have half as many books available as do schools in wealthier communities (Guice et al., 1996; Krashen, 1993; McQuillan, 1998).

Now some of this discrepancy is related to inequities in education funding patterns (Kozol, 1991) but some is also related to local decisions on how funds will be spent. For instance, schools in lower-income communities have smaller school and classroom libraries but employ far more paraprofessionals than schools in wealthier communities. Personally, if I were working in a high-poverty school and had to choose between spending $12,000 each year on more books for classrooms and libraries or on one more paraprofessional for the building, I would opt for the books. Especially given the research on the positive impact of book access and the negative or, at best, neutral, evidence on the effects of paraprofessionals on children's reading achievement (Allington & Cunningham, 2001).

Children from lower-income homes especially need rich and extensive collections of books in the school library and in their classrooms if only because these are the children least likely to have a supply of books at home.

But for libraries to be truly useful their books and staff must be available on an "as-needed" basis as recommended by the American Library Association in its recent publication, *Information Power: Building Partnerships for Learning.* This publication also recommends before- and after-school access to the library, especially necessary in schools where many children have few books or other information resources at home. Two primary roles of the library media specialist are: (1) linking library resources to the core curriculum for teachers and students and (2) helping students find just the right book to satisfy their current curiosity or literacy needs. Paraprofessionals or student volunteers can check out books for children. They can reshelve books that have been returned. They can stamp new books and enter them into the cataloging database. Librarians should be free to act on their expertise, not saddled with clerking duties.

The school library is important. Too many schools libraries have been underfunded so that collections are undersized and the facility is understaffed. In these schools, children typically have very restricted access to library collections, perhaps visiting only once a week and restricted to a single book exchange (Guice et al., 1996). As McQuillan (1998) so powerfully demonstrates, library adequacy is among the better predictors of reading achievement with a correlation of .85 between library adequacy and NAEP reading achievement scores. In other words, you could quite accurately rank the states' NAEP scores just by knowing their ranking on school library quality.

School Book Rooms.   A more recent development for enhancing children's access to appropriate books is the "school book room" (Fountas & Pinnell, 1999). Such rooms house supplies of books that classroom teachers may "check out" for use in their classroom. I have encountered several schemes for school book rooms but the basic scheme is always the same—providing a larger "library-like" supply of books for classroom use. This design provides a wider

Books at Home and School

A recent study (Smith et al., 1993) recorded the numbers of children's books available in the homes and classrooms located in schools in three different communities. Their findings point to the enormous inequity in access to books that exists in the United States.

	Books at home	*In classroom library*
Middle income	199	392
Lower income	2.6	54
Lowest income	.4	47

This is one of the six shelves of copies of circulating instructional texts in a Texas school's book room.

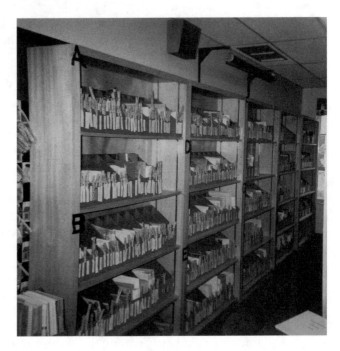

access at lower expense than traditional plans that purchased multiple copies of identical books for each classroom.

In the basic school book room, you would likely find multiple copies of leveled books (Fountas & Pinnell, 1999; Mace, 1997). These leveled books are typically stored in magazine sleeves or specially designed little book boxes or bins and arranged on shelves by difficulty level. Typically, ten to fifteen copies of a single title are stored in each box or bin and teachers check out sets of books, often limited to no more than five copies of any given book at a time. This means several teachers can have access to copies of the same titles simultaneously. Of course, when starting a school book room, you need to decide whether to begin by ordering five copies of three different books or fifteen copies of a single book. I always vote for the former and then add additional copies of high-demand titles over time.

A fully stocked school book room would have a collection of books that spanned the grades in the school. In addition, in some school book rooms there are also available bins of books organized by genre, author, or topic. These bins are typically multilevel (except, perhaps in the case of single author bins) and linked to science, social studies, and language arts curriculum goals. For instance, a school book room in Texas contained bins of books on the Alamo, biographies of famous Texans, Native American histories in the Southwest, the Rio Grande, and so on. Teachers could check out any of these bins to support social studies lessons and to provide additional social studies reading materials at various levels of difficulty.

In a California school book room there were bins of books organized by genre—following the districts English Language Arts curriculum plan. Thus, fifth-grade teachers who were working to develop an understanding of the genre of biography could check out this biography bin and have available another thirty to forty biographies for students to select from as they read the required three to four biographies for the unit.

In Wisconsin a school book room had bins of books for author studies, again so that students would have opportunities to read multiple books by the selected authors. Thus, there were bins filled with books by Donald Crews, Judy Blume, Mildred Taylor, Russell Freedman, and many other authors. When teachers decided to focus on the work, the style, or the themes of a single author they could draw from over thirty bins of books. Each author bin typically contained one or two copies of multiple titles by that author.

The school book room is a wonderful innovation but it does take collaborative planning and a sense of sharing. In planning purchases, schools need to take the long view and not attempt to stock the book room all at once. A five-year plan seems appropriate for bringing the book room up to speed but every annual budget should have some money allocated to book room purchasing every year forevermore (there is always wear and tear and always good new texts available).

Once the book room has been stocked, especially initially, there have to be guidelines for how much material any one teacher can have checked out at any given time and guidelines on how long materials are to be kept before they are returned to the book room shelves (or how long another teacher must wait for them to be returned). In most book rooms I have seen teachers put a snap clothespin (with their name on it) on the book sleeve they have selected books from, or on the shelf where the book bin they are using was stored. This alerts other teachers about who has what and allows for informal negotiations about usage.

Remember that everyone cannot have the biography bin out at the same time (nor the Iroquois bin or the Arnold Lobel bin). Thus, some collaborative planning is needed ahead of time. Everyone can still teach the biography unit, but everyone cannot teach it the same month and use the single biography bin.

However, the cost savings can be substantial if teachers can agree to work within a school book room plan. For instance, consider the biography unit. If biography is a fourth-grade curriculum goal and a school has five fourth-grade teachers, then developing a single bin of forty biographies costs the same as giving each teacher eight copies of the same biography or one copy of eight biographies. In neither case will any teacher have anything but a very minimal collection of biographies. On the other hand, to provide each teacher with forty biographies of their own would cost five times as much. If each biography, in paperback, could be purchased for an average cost of five dollars, then the single bin costs about $200 whereas it would cost $1,000.00 to put the same forty titles in every classroom.

While forty biographies may not be a sufficient number to actually satisfy the reading needs of a diverse class of 4th graders, such a collection has a chance

---

A New Zealand Perspective

The author is a program coordinator with *The Learning Network,* a national school reform and teacher development effort sponsored by Richard C. Owen publishers. In this short piece she describes some of the surprises she encountered after she arrived from New Zealand and first began working in American elementary schools.

"Teachers who had a set of books referred to them as "my books" because they had been allocated the money to purchase them [or had purchased the books themselves]. One New York teacher who had changed to a lower grade level had no books in her room when she arrived. She was expected to buy them herself or scrounge from other teachers who were reluctant to part with any of theirs … In New Zealand the school takes full responsibility for the purchase of instructional texts." (Mace, 1997, p. 276)

---

of putting at least some appropriate biographies in every child's hands (and desk). And there is still the school library collection to draw biographies from.

Some school book rooms also have bins containing twenty to thirty-plus copies, or class sets, of selected titles—a few titles that all children will be expected to read. For reasons that should be obvious at this point, I am not a big fan of class sets—or of curriculum plans that insist on all children reading the same book. Nonetheless, the school book room is useful when such plans are in use. As in the above biography unit example, schools can purchase a single class set that rotates among teachers following that curriculum plan. And, again, it works as long as everyone does not plan to teach with the same class set during the same week- or two-week period. Such a scheme means buying fewer class sets, which should make funds for better stocking of classroom collections and school book rooms with multiple titles!

Personally, it seems to me that teachers should expect to have a sufficient supply of books available in their classrooms to teach the children they are assigned. In other words, if a fifth-grade class has some lower-achieving students, perhaps reading at a beginning-third-grade level, then it would seem the basic responsibility of the school to ensure that the classroom book and curriculum materials collections were stocked with an ample array of third-grade-level, or below, texts linked to core curriculum standards for fifth-grade students.

It has long puzzled me why the adequacy of school libraries and classroom book collections are not a key topic in teacher labor agreement negotiations. Similarly, I have wondered why the appropriateness of the curriculum materials isn't more often a negotiable item. I will assert that the research points to the importance of easy access to appropriate texts as at least as important as the number of minutes of planning time allocated, class size, and length of the school day—all issues regularly negotiated in teacher contracts.

Magazines?   Adults spend substantially more time reading magazines and newspapers than books. But magazines are not often found in classrooms even though there are, perhaps, a hundred or so magazines published for children and adolescents. Stoll (1997) provides a comprehensive listing (and ordering information) of magazine titles. In an ideal world, schools might supply every child with one or more magazine subscriptions of their choice in order to level the playing field.

Currently, children from wealthier homes are far more likely to have one or more magazines delivered to their homes each month. And the NAEP survey indicated that the only group of fourth graders who achieved reading performances above the national average were those who indicated that they regularly read story books, informational books, *and magazines* (Foertsch, 1992). Many schools have library subscriptions to a variety of magazines (although, again, schools in low-income neighborhoods have far fewer subscriptions than wealthier schools) but often these magazines are not allowed to leave the library.

A rich classroom magazine supply should become a staple in elementary school classrooms. *Ranger Rick, National Geographic Geo, Cobblestone,* and *Sports Illustrated for Kids* are but a few of the popular children's magazines that I would recommend for every intermediate-grade classroom. These magazines should become part and parcel of the reading material that children have access to during self-selected reading periods and to take home for weekend reading activity.

One school I visited recently placed magazine racks in every toilet stall. Talk about authentic reading! But the goal was simply to entice kids to pick up

---

Magazines for Children and Adolescents
(That You May Never Have Heard of)

Ages 6–11	Ages 8–14	Ages 14 and up
American Girl	*Calliope*	*Blue Jean*
Barbie	*Cracked*	*Dramatics*
Black Belt for Kids	*Earthsavers*	*Freeway*
Chickadee	*Hip*	*Karate/Kung Fu*
Dolphin Log	*Koala Club*	*Lefthander*
Kid City	*Metrokids*	*ScienceWorld*
Nickelodeon	*Otterwise*	*Slap*
Owl	*Racing for kids*	*Teen*
Skipping Stones	*Soccer Jr.*	*Teen People*
Stone Soup	*Sports Illustrated, Kids*	*Newsweek for teens*
Zoobooks	*Teen Beat*	*YM*

Information on each of the magazines can be found in Stoll's (1997) compilation *Magazines for Kids and Teens* (International Reading Association, www.reading.org).

reading materials and take a look. If students seemed to take a while in the restroom, it was usually because they had found a magazine story of interest.

In an ideal world we might also attempt to level the literacy playing field by making one or two magazine subscriptions available to every student. In other words, each student would be offered a choice of several magazines they could regularly receive, free of charge. The magazines might even be delivered to the students' homes. Yes, such an initiative would cost between $25 and $35 per student. But that is .007 percent of the $5,000 average per-pupil expenditure in the United States.

Series Books, Junk Reading.   There is another often underappreciated genre of reading material that we need to consider when rethinking children's access to books they can read easily, fluently, and with understanding. These are the often maligned series books. Without getting too technical, I have defined series books as those books that either (1) have continuing characters (e.g., *Nancy Drew, Arthur, Harry Potter*) or (2) are predictable in plot and story line even though the characters change (*Goosebumps, Choose Your Own Adventure*). Some series books are viewed as having more literary merit and some sell by the millions regardless of their literary merit. But as a group, series books have been largely shunned by the commercial anthologies, the literary awards committees, and local curriculum developers. This seems a shame since so many adult avid readers recall those first series books that hooked them into reading.

Egoff (1972) captured what seems to me to be a prevailing sentiment among many educators. "Perhaps mediocre books do no harm in the sense of actual damage. But they do harm in the sense of deprivation—the subtraction of opportunity to know and experience the best" (p. 10). Her argument is that

Here are some of the numerous emerging reader series available today.

since time is a finite variable, time spent reading "mediocre" books, and she does not limit mediocrity to series books (in her view only 2½% of all published children's books are of excellent literary quality), limits the time available to read the quality literature. While I believe I understand her concern, I simply do not agree with the argument.

In fact, I would argue that it may be the time spent reading series books, and even other mediocre books, that creates the skill and interest in reading the better-quality books. I do think that adults, including teachers, have an obligation to help children find quality books to read but we must also, and perhaps first, help children find out why to read and how to read.

Here is my hypothesis about series books and their potential role in reading development, especially in the transitional years (grades 2–6). I think series books are enjoyable because the characters are a bit flat, the plots a bit too predictable, and the settings too familiar. These, of course, are the sorts of criticisms leveled at series books by those promoting the reading of quality books. But imagine how difficult it must be for some children, maybe many children, to understand the larger skills of plot development, character development, perspective taking, and so on when we feed them a steady diet of (1) excerpted

These books represent only a small part of the series book collections published for the early elementary grade reader (although many of the titles are appropriate for older elementary readers also).

materials in an anthology or (2) high-quality children's books, representing a variety of genres, authors, literary styles, plot structures, and characters.

I will suggest that reading a half-dozen *Boxcar Children* books, or *Encyclopedia Brown* books, or *Polk Street School* books, or even *Baby Sitters Club* books, may actually make acquiring these "higher-order" literacy skills easier. After a couple of books, the central characters become familiar, predictable. It is easier to predict how DW will respond after having read three *Arthur* books, which means that you have read a lot about DW and her relationship with her brother. Likewise, after a couple of *Polk Street School* books, Richard Best, the "beast" in Mrs. Rooney's room, becomes a familiar presence. Suddenly it is easier to think about who in your classroom reminds you of DW or Richard and to tell why. After a half-dozen *Arthur* books it becomes even easier to answer the question: What would DW do?

Of course, series books also simplify the reading act by reducing the word recognition load, particularly proper nouns (e.g., characters, locations). Unlike the traditional reading anthology that provides primarily excerpts from books, thus offering a plethora of new names and places, series books offer a comfortably familiar vocabulary. But series books also offer a commonality in text structure—or author's style. All of this seems to work to make the books more readable as each one is completed.

So let's add series books to our classrooms. Let's promote series books by reading them aloud once in awhile. Let's have kids share their favorite series. Maybe even help organize student "clubs" promoting particular series across classrooms and even across grade levels. Some series books seem to have a substantial "reach." *Babysitters Club*, *Star Wars*, *Dear America*, and *Goosebumps* books, for instance, are popular from around the end of third grade well up into the middle grades. Celebrate series books even if you don't include them in the official curriculum.

There is a concern that we must attend to, however. As in so many other aspects of schools, children who come from wealthier families are those most

---

Popular Series Books for the Transition Years

Greg Brooks and I have surveyed approximately 1,000 teachers in ten states. Below are the series that these teachers most frequently report their students love.

Primary Grades	*Intermediate Grades*
Arthur	Goosebumps
Frog and Toad	Babysitter's Club
Clifford	Boxcar Children
Cam Jansen	Animorphs
Henry and Mudge	American Girl

As elementary students mature in both the reading proficiency and social arenas, the topics of series books available become more mature and also more specific.

likely to have read series books. This is because paperback book sales are largely a middle-class phenomenon. According to a recent study conducted by the American Booksellers Association, 70 percent of juvenile books are purchased by families with incomes above $30,000.

It is the grocery stores in middle-class neighborhoods that allocate shelf space to books, and for kids' books that shelf space is almost always space for series books. It is the mall bookstores that offer series books galore—the middle-class mall. It is in middle-class schools that the mail-order book clubs thrive (Strickland & Walmsley, 1993). As teachers in lower-income schools find few orders coming in they often stop distributing the order flyers. It becomes too emotionally draining to hear children continuing to imagine which books they *would* order if they had any money to order a book.

Putting Books in Their Bedrooms. While I think we must first be concerned with children's access to books at school, I also think we must become more concerned about ensuring children's access to appropriate books outside of school. There are several possibilities to consider. First, schools might participate in an inexpensive book distribution program. These efforts focus on providing all children with books, typically at no charge to the child or family.

The Reading is Fundamental (RIF) program was designed to put no-cost books into the hands of children from low-income families. In many respects RIF has been incredibly successful but RIF reaches so few poor children and provides those it reaches with so few books that it seems, at best, a drop in the bucket of needs. RIF currently funds few new projects because much of the available funding is already allocated to existing projects. But there is a stupendous need for a broader, wider RIF-like program. Another option for inexpensive books is the Reading Recycling Project (www.literacyempowerment.org/lef/recycling.html).

Book Stamps

Sen. Edward Kennedy has introduced federal legislation that would provide children from low-income families with book stamps that would be exchangeable for books at book fairs and bookstores. I hope this effort, which is modeled after the federal Food Stamp program, is funded.

This nonprofit distributes new and used books free of charge (recipients pay shipping and handling). No specific titles can be ordered but the application form asks for information on the kids that will be receiving the books. The same group offers a "books below cost" option. Here there is a $48.00 charge for twenty-five titles but you get new books and can select the sets you want.

All children deserve books of their own. All children deserve bedroom libraries where they have at least a handful of books of their own. We are a wealthy nation and we can afford to provide all children with a few books of their own. Finding funding for such a venture may not be as difficult as you think. Potential donors seem to understand the importance of books of one's own.

For instance, the Moncure Elementary School in Stafford (VA) operates a "Book for a Buck" program two mornings a week. Here students can purchase used books and some new books for 25 cents, 50 cents, or a dollar. Student cashiers staff the bookstore. The used-book titles primarily come from donations that are solicited community-wide and from books purchased at garage sales with the small profits made.

Schools make choices about how available funds will be spent. What if schools spent as much money on providing children with books of their own as they now spend providing children with workbooks of their own (phonics workbooks, spelling workbooks, math workbooks, reading workbooks, penmanship workbooks, test prep workbooks, etc.)? In at least one school district putting books in students' hands is seen as important.

In the Sweet Home Public Schools (NY), all students, K–12, were provided with a $25.00 gift certificate worth $33.00 toward the purchase of books at participating bookstores (with the arranged discount). The assistant superintendent who championed the project said, "We spend thousands of dollars per pupil in this district. If I cannot convince the taxpayers that this small allocation per child is a worthy investment, I shouldn't be an assistant superintendent."

Building and Displaying the Classroom Collections.   You will need a general plan to redesign your school program based on the reliable, replicated scientific research that shows the critical importance of providing kids with easy access to books they can read accurately, fluently, and with understanding. You know you will need to begin the process of thinking about what sorts of books will be ordered for the classroom collections in the initial year. You know you need

This Illinois teacher has organized this section of her classroom library into bins of books representing both types of books and favorite series books.

to develop a plan for ordering books within certain ranges of complexity and develop a schoolwide procedure for identifying the difficulty of the books ordered. You also need to plan for the school book room, which will need shelving and storage boxes and bins and a schoolwide procedure for sharing the books across the year and throughout the school.

But there is one more concern that needs attention. Where do you put all the books in the classroom? How do you make the books accessible and visible to children? Well, the worst plan is to put the books on shelves with their spines facing out. This makes the books less accessible simply because you have to work so hard to find a book you might want to read.

Two broad approaches have demonstrated value for enhancing children's access to the book collections. First, create classroom displays and change them frequently. These might be author displays or genre displays or topic displays. I might walk into a fourth-grade classroom in New York State and see a collection of two dozen or more books on the Hudson River, a theme in social studies, displayed on top of a book shelf at eyeball height. Some of the books are from the school library, a couple are from the classroom collection, but most

This young man seems entranced by this book from his favorite series (although the *Captain Underpants* series runs a close second).

are from the Hudson River book bin kept in the school book room. On a flat wire rack there is a display of fables, for the current language arts focus, with their covers visible. On a small table there is a display of books by Jean George who will be featured next month in language arts in an author study. The children can select any of her books to read now to begin to develop a familiarity with her style, her craft, her works. But many more of her titles will be added to the display in a few weeks.

On the teacher's desk is a small stack of books that she will "bless" today (Gambrell, 1997). These blessings are blessedly brief, just a few seconds each. The teacher holds up the book and mentions the title and offers a few words of information or response to the book and then moves on to another. She may mention that the book offers information on a topic they will be studying or was written by an author they know. Or she may simply say something like, "If you like scary books/funny books/sports stories this book may be for you." For some books she may read just a bit of it. Others may have the illustrations exhibited. The goal here is to offer children a quick introduction—something to entice them to read these books. So each day, each teacher picks a few books, 5–10, from the milieu to feature. This helps ensure that children notice the range of books available. It works to entice the child who would not search the collection very long for a book to read. Or at least wouldn't when he began the school year.

Summary

Kids not only need to read a lot but they also need lots of books they can read right at their fingertips. They also need access to books that entice them, attract them to reading. Schools can foster wider reading by creating school and classroom collections that provide a rich and wide array of appropriate books and magazines and by providing time every day for children to actually sit and read. They can make it easy and unrisky for children to take books home for the evening or weekend by worrying less about losing books to children and more about losing children to illiteracy.

But the emphasis must first be on ensuring abundant reading opportunities during the school day. We need to create school literacy programs and environments that entice children and adolescents to take our books home to read on their own time. The research suggests only a limited impact for mandated reading at home—homework reading—while providing tantalizing support for efforts that enhance the volume of voluntary reading that children do.

I must also admit that when I walk into a lower-achieving school and see a library with few books and student access restricted to a single weekly visit and I see classrooms with few books and no book displays, I am dismayed. When I see remedial rooms and special education rooms filled with workbooks and with computers that offer electronic workbooks, I cringe. When I see little time allocated for just reading but find a mandate that parents read with their children every evening, I get angry over such "blame the victim" policies. In these situations I wonder just how the folks who run this school got so far off track. How is it that in such schools there is money for paraprofessionals in every classroom, for a home-school coordinator, for an assistant principal, for a social worker, for a gifted coordinator, for an in-school suspension supervisor, and so on, but no damn money for books? All too frequently I enter schools where I find it hard to imagine that any but the most determined child will ever learn to read given the mindless decisions the adults have made about spending the money available. Schools without rich supplies of engaging, accessible, appropriate books are not schools that are likely to teach many children to read at all, much less develop thoughtful literacy in most students.

4

KIDS NEED TO LEARN TO READ FLUENTLY

There are several observable behaviors that accompany difficult reading. One of the most obvious is a slowing of reading rate. This is often accompanied by finger pointing, even in adults. Often the phrasing and intonation breaks down. Rereading of a passage or a segment of the passage is another signal. Rereading occurs when we recognize that our reading seems to have gone off track and the text is not making sense to us. If we routinely monitored signs of anxiety or stress, we would find that hard reading, particularly reading that is not making sense, increases bodily signs of anxiety, a physiological signal of frustration (Johnston, 1985). The difficulty we experience may come from a lack of familiarity with the topic being presented, which may lead to difficulty with word pronunciation as well as the ability to understand the word meanings. The difficulty may stem from poorly organized information (think of the directions accompanying your income tax forms or your software program). When our motivation is high, we will typically persist with difficult reading (Wigfield, 1997). But when motivation and interest are low, we often simply terminate the reading activity—sometimes with obvious symptoms of frustration.

A key point to understand is that everyone encounters texts that present difficulties. And everyone responds to difficult texts in predictable ways. Beginning readers seem almost to necessarily move through this word-by-word, fingerpointing stage (Biemiller, 1970; Weber, 1970) before moving on to a more fluent reading style. But some children's reading continues to routinely exhibit these signals (e.g., finger pointing, word-by-word reading, lack of self-monitoring, anxiety) even when the topic is familiar and word pronunciation and familiarity pose no particular problems. Often these children have a historical pattern of slower development of reading proficiencies. These children are often those served by any of the several instructional support programs (remedial reading, resource room). In this chapter, the primary focus is on fostering more fluent reading in these struggling readers.

UNDERSTANDING THE IMPORTANCE OF READING FLUENTLY

While there has been much research on the role of reading accuracy in reading development (see Allington, 1984), far less work has examined the development of reading fluency. Fluency, in beginning reading, has been measured, historically, primarily by recording oral reading rate. The *Gray Standardized Oral Reading Paragraphs* (1915) began this tradition by providing reading rate criteria to determine the adequacy of an oral reading performance. More recently, the American Federation of Teachers (1999, p. 20) suggests establishing minimum reading rate goals. In many respects, reading rate is a general measure of fluency in that word-by-word reading is always slower than reading in phrases. Reading without rereading is always faster than reading with rereading necessitated by difficulties in making sense out of the material being read.

But it isn't just fast reading that is the issue here. Fluent reading is faster but there are other features to consider as well. Clay and Imlach (1971) conducted the classic study on the development of reading fluency. They examined the reading behaviors of 100 beginning readers and noted that those early readers making the greatest progress not only read faster and more accurately but also with better phrasing and intonation. While the lowest-progress readers read aloud in one and two word segments, the highest-progress readers read in five to seven word phrases. Of course, reading in phrases produced faster reading as well. The high-progress readers also spontaneously self-corrected four and five times as many of their word pronunciation errors as did the lower-progress readers. Thus, these two characteristics, phrase reading with appropriate intonation and spontaneous self-correction of many misread words, were clearly associated with those children making better progress in learning to read. However, because it is so difficult to study such subtle linguistic features of reading, most other researchers interested in the development of fluency have focused on reading rate, an easily measured factor, rather than on measures of juncture, prosody, intonation, and stress.

Reading-rate research shows a steady increase in the numbers of words read per minute (wpm), the most common rate measure, as children progress through school. The increases are larger in the elementary years than in the middle and high school years (Rasinski, 2000). Reading rate is related to reading volume because children with slower rates simply read fewer words than faster readers in the same amount of time. At the intermediate grades, for instance, one child may finish *Stone Fox* in a little more than an hour (reading at around 200 wpm), while it may take another slower-reading child almost three hours (at 75 wpm). In such cases, social studies reading, science reading, and even math reading will also take the slower reading child much longer to complete. Slower reading means that some children may read far less even when given the same amount of time as other children. And as was noted in chapter 2, volume of reading matters in reading development. And the slower rate, limited self-monitoring, and lack of fluency often predict reading that has gone off track in terms of comprehension. Thus, even though the reader spends longer reading, lower comprehension is the end result.

But we cannot get too carried away with a focus on reading rate. I do think the development of reading fluency and rate needs to be monitored and when children deviate enormously and regularly from general adequacy standards we need to explore the issue further. What I worry the most about is the

Reading Rates

Harris and Sipay (1990) present a summary of information on reading rates established on several standardized reading rate measures. The chart below was developed from those data.

General range of adequate reading rates by grade levels

Grade	WPM	Grade	WPM
1	60–90	6	195–220
2	85–120	7	215–245
3	115–140	8	235–270
4	140–170	9	250–270
5	170–195	12	250–300

Reading rate guidelines must be applied with caution because a number of factors will influence rate. For instance, oral reading is slower than silent reading. The reading rates for younger children are typically established from oral reading activity while the rates for older children are established from silent reading activity. But younger children may exhibit little difference in oral and silent reading rates, while for older students that gap should be quite substantial.

possibility that we literally teach some children slow reading and the slow reading becomes a habit.

LaBerge and Samuels (1974) linked the concept of "automaticity" to the development of proficient reading. At its simplest, automaticity refers to the ability to engage and coordinate a number of complex subskills and strategies with little cognitive effort. For instance, as children develop as readers an increasingly larger number of words are recognized with little effort—that is, without much, if any, conscious attention to the word structure. This is not quite the same as "sight word" reading because some of the words are decoded quickly using larger word patterns instead of a process of letter-by-letter analysis (Share & Stanovich, 1995). Reading fluently requires automatic information processing.

But some children seem to be able to read with a high degree of accuracy yet still do not read fluently—that is, with phrasing and intonation. This word-by-word reading limits their rate of reading and, in many cases, has a negative impact on comprehension. Just why this developmental lag occurs is not well understood (Allington, 1983).

Several hypotheses have been advanced, however. One suggests that since some children come to school having had few books read to them, compared to other children, these limited experiences may negatively impact the development of reading fluency. However, studies that provide struggling readers with a fluent reader model (through tape recordings or teacher read-aloud models) offer only mixed support for developing fluent reading. Dowhower (1987) and Rasinski (1990) compared assisted repeated reading (teacher providing a model of fluent reading) with unassisted repeated reading (students simply reread passages with no model) on second- and third-grade students. Both reported that similar results were produced by either technique although Dowhower suggested some improvements in intonation and prosody for the assisted group. Overall, however, both techniques improved students' general reading rate, accuracy, and comprehension. It may be that there are some children who benefit more than others from the modeling of fluent reading. On the one hand, in the studies available, results are reported for the group and the groups of children, on average, did not much benefit from having the model available. On the other hand, no study reported any negative effects of providing a fluent reader model and there is modest evidence of a small positive effect.

These studies represent but two of the more comprehensive studies of the impact of repeated reading on reading fluency and comprehension. Other studies have demonstrated that repeated reading is more effective than listening to stories repeatedly, than practicing rapid word recognition of passage words on word lists or flashcards, and compared to providing students with indications of where phrase boundaries are located in the text they are asked to read (e.g., Dahl, 1977; Herman, 1985; O'Shea, Sindelar, & O'Shea, 1985; Rashotte & Torgeson, 1985). The evidence available provides reliable and replicated scientific evidence of the positive impact of repeated readings on a variety of reading tasks and outcome measures. These studies also indicate that engaging children in repeated readings of a text is particularly effective in fostering more fluent reading in children struggling to develop proficient reading strategies (Samuels, Schermer, & Reinking, 1992).

There is another hypothesis as to why some children can read texts reasonably accurately but with little fluency. In this case, word-by-word reading may be a learned adaptive response to a specific type of instructional setting (Allington, 1983). Children read word-by-word when they have learned to rely primarily on an external monitor (the teacher, aide, or other students) when reading aloud. So how is this dependence learned?

Research has demonstrated that teachers are more likely to have lower-achieving readers read aloud than the better readers (Allington, 1983; Chinn et al., 1993; Collins, 1986). Often this reading aloud occurs during a traditional "round robin" reading activity where each child reads aloud a bit, in turn. During this activity teachers are far more likely to interrupt the lower-achieving readers than the higher-achieving readers, regardless of the quality of errors, and to interrupt poor readers more quickly and to have the interruption focus on "sounding words out" (Allington, 1980; Chinn et al., 1993; Hoffman et al., 1984). In addition, teachers allow other children to interrupt struggling readers, while discouraging such interruptions when better readers read aloud (Eder & Felmlee, 1984).

Thus, struggling readers are:

- more likely to be reading material that is difficult for them,
- more likely to be asked to read aloud,
- more likely to be interrupted when they miscall a word,
- more likely to be interrupted more quickly,

- more likely to pause and wait for a teacher to prompt, and
- more likely to be told to sound out a word.

While better readers are:

- more likely to be reading material of appropriate difficulty,
- more likely to be asked to read silently,
- more likely to be expected to self-monitor and self-correct,
- more likely to be interrupted only after a wait period or at end of sentence, and
- more likely to be asked to reread or to cross-check when interrupted.

In the face of such different reading lessons, it isn't surprising that struggling readers begin to read hesitantly. I describe the word-by-word behavior as a learned "checking the traffic" response. When struggling readers grow used to a steady stream of rapid, external interruptions, they begin to read with an anticipation of interruptions—word-by-word. At the extreme you can hear children pausing after each word while awaiting the teacher's confirmation of a correct pronunciation. On some of the audiotapes of struggling readers reading aloud (to an aide, their classroom teacher, or resource teacher) there is an audible, "Um-huh" from the teacher after every word is pronounced by the struggling readers. In some severe cases, the struggling reader actually looks up from the text to check with the teacher after every word is read.

But this is a trained behavior, not an indication of anything else in particular. Some have thought that word-by-word reading suggests an inadequate sight vocabulary or limited decoding proficiency. But there have been a number of studies indicating that struggling older readers, those word-by-word readers, when compared to reading-level matched younger readers often know more sight words and have more phonics skills than those younger better readers. But the younger better readers read more fluently and with better self-monitoring (Allington, 1984). Other studies have shown that training struggling readers to recognize words faster had little positive effect on reading fluency or overall reading achievement (Dahl, 1977).

What does seem effective is providing struggling readers with lots of opportunities to develop self-monitoring skills and strategies (Samuels, Schermer & Reinking, 1992): providing repeated reading with limited, if any, interruptions while the child reads.

A final hypothesis on why some children don't develop adequate fluency or rate of reading is quite simple: They have had limited reading practice in appropriately leveled materials. I know of no research testing this hypothesis. Perhaps this is because designing such a study—at least one following the REA criteria for scientific research—would create some ethical concerns. That is, given the known power of placing children in appropriately leveled text, providing a steady diet of hard texts to some randomly selected children while providing a steady diet of appropriate texts to other randomly selected children would seem to violate the basic ethical principle of "Knowingly, do no harm." It would also seem that this would be a difficult situation in which it would be difficult to get parents' voluntary informed consent.

Lots of practice, including repeated readings of favorite texts, are important in the development of fluency.

Nonetheless, the widespread evidence that struggling readers are often placed in texts that are too hard (given the level of support available) and the commonness of fluency problems in these students suggests that the "checking the traffic" hypothesis deserves consideration. I do know from my clinical experiences that providing children access with appropriately leveled texts and a noninterruptive reading environment typically produces profound changes in reading fluency and self-monitoring. But designing such lessons is the topic of the next section.

INTERVENTIONS TO DEVELOP FLUENCY IN STRUGGLING READERS

A number of intervention strategies have been studied with a variety of specific instructional strategies that have demonstrated effectiveness in developing fluency and, concurrently, fostering comprehension. In this section, the most successful strategies are reviewed in three clusters. Tutorial approaches, small group approaches, and an approach that requires whole-class instructional redesign.

Tutorial Approaches

Much of the available research used tutorial interventions to foster improved reading fluency (and the accompanying growth in rate, comprehension, and volume of reading). Tutorial approaches could be offered in the classroom or in a resource room. The intervention can be delivered by the classroom teacher, a specialist teacher, a trained paraprofessional or adult volunteer, or even by an older student in a peer tutoring plan. There are no studies that actually compare the potentially differing effects that might occur based on who delivered the instructional support and virtually all studies report a facilitative impact on fluency regardless of who leads the tutorial intervention. Nonetheless, I will suggest that the more expert the tutor the greater the likelihood of progress in the greatest number of struggling readers. Thus, whenever possible, tutorial support should be offered by teachers, ideally, by expert teachers.

The very first step I recommend is a schoolwide training effort, including anyone who might be listening to struggling readers read aloud—even if no fluency tutorial, per se, is planned. The training would simply focus on a set of procedures for responding when readers produce a mispronunciation or simply stop while reading aloud. The training is intended to heighten awareness of the use of interruptive responses and the potential that such interruptive responding has on the development of readers who rely on an external source to monitor their reading. The most effective training package that I have used is a short video entitled *Peer Power* (Richard C. Owen Publisher, 914–232–3903) that provides training for paired reading tutors.

Paired Reading Peer Tutors.   In this video, children are provided a *Preview-Pause-Prompt-Praise* (PPPP) strategy. This paired-reading peer-tutoring technique has been popularized by Keith Topping (1987, Topping & Ehly, 1998), who has evaluated this procedure in a number of sites in Great Britain. These evaluations and a number of others point to the positive effects this strategy has on developing fluency and general reading achievement. The basic procedure presented in the training video is: *Preview*, the tutor simply engages the child in a very brief discussion of the title and cover art focusing on the question, "What do you think this story is about?" Then the tutor and the tutee begin reading aloud together. When the tutee wishes to read alone, he or she simply taps the table or desk and the tutor allows him or her to continue on alone. However, if the tutee stumbles or misreads the text, the tutor will *Pause*, and, literally, count to three silently or wait until the tutee reaches the end of the sentence. This provides the reader with an opportunity to self-correct, work through the decoding of the word, reread the sentence, or to use other powerful strategies associated with good readers. If, after the pause, the reader has not self-corrected, not figured out the word, or not yet responded, *Prompt* helpfully and strategically. Now this can be the complicated part. A usual first prompt is, "Let's read that again." If the misreading is not corrected or if the tutee still fails to pronounce the word, the tutor then provides the pronunciation and begins to read along with the tutee again. If the tutee self-corrects or figures out the word, the tutor offers *Praise* for the reading strategy used and then begins to read with the tutee again until the tutee taps on the table. After reading, the tutor offers praise for the use of good reading strategies and then simply requests that the tutee, "Tell me your favorite part of the story." After the response, the tutor shares a favorite part also.

This rather simple strategy can be profitably used by virtually anyone who listens to children read. This assisted reading helps smooth out choppy word-by-word reading while at the same time supporting better self-monitoring and improved accuracy.

I recommend that parents and paraprofessionals, as well as teachers and peers, use a similar strategy when they listen to children read aloud. It seems important, if the goal is eliminating the reliance on an external monitor, that virtually all reading aloud that a student might do would support the development of self-monitoring and fluent reading. If the PPPP strategy is implemented only occasionally, progress toward fluent reading might be hampered. Thus, providing training opportunities to paraprofessionals, peers, and parents is also needed.

Tape, Check, Chart.   Another simple individual procedure is the use of audiotape recordings. However, in this case, the students audiotape their own reading. After the first reading, they replay the tape while following along with the text (actually a photocopy of the text works best). As they listen, students attempt to mark all the mispronunciations they produced in black ink (just placing a small check above all mispronounced words). Then they read it again and again tape record the reading. Again they listen to the tape, they again mark all mispronunciations on the same copy of the text, this time with a red pen (or blue or green). Finally, they read the text a third time and again listen and mark the misreads in a different ink. Students can tally and chart the number of mispronunciations made on each reading. Typically, each rereading produces fewer misread words and each reread sounds better—more fluent. The error-marking procedure makes this progress readily visible to the reader.

Tape, Time, Chart.   A related strategy has the student read a text aloud several times, each time recording how long it takes to complete the passage (in seconds, usually). The times can also be recorded and charted. This requires a simple stopwatch (trying to record time from a classroom clock does not work very well). Again, typically each rereading takes less time and the students can observe their own progress.

But remember that proficient reading is more than fast reading. While fluency practice and monitoring reading rate are useful techniques, the goal isn't just faster more fluent oral reading. The goal is improved comprehension of the material read and, perhaps, an improved confidence that reading can be: (1) improved and (2) an enjoyable personal experience. After repeated failure, some children benefit greatly from the simple signs of progress, fewer misread words or increased speed, that come from repeated readings (or assisted reading).

Older Kids, Baby Books.   One problem we have encountered, particularly in the upper grades, is that some struggling readers need really easy texts to practice on but easy books are stigmatized. In other words, these sixth graders reading at a second-grade level don't want to be caught dead with a copy of a *PeeWee Scouts* book in their possession. It is not hard to understand their reluctance to stick a beginning reader book in their back pocket.

But what if they are using that *PeeWee Scouts* book in a peer tutoring arrangement with a third-grade struggling reader? Now the focus becomes one of reading the book so they can help their tutee. Often this is just the sort of arrangement that allows older elementary (and middle school and even high school) students to work with easy texts without feeling wholly inadequate.

Small Group Approaches

Several studies have examined the impact of small group interventions on the development of reading fluency and comprehension. These can be offered in the classroom or in special programs.

Choral Reading.   An age-old technique is choral reading, or having all of the students in a group read aloud together. Usually the teacher leads the choral reading activity. Typically the choral reading occurs after the teacher has already read the text with the students following along or after the students have read the story silently. The choral reading activity does not require reading the whole story aloud. In fact, often just segments are practiced this way. Teachers might select particular segments for different reasons.

Teachers might select a passage that is central to understanding the plot. Or a segment that includes dialogue (if helping readers better read dialogue aloud is the goal). Or perhaps a segment where tone and voice seems important (a scary segment that deserves to be read in a whisper, for instance). The key feature is the fluent reading that is practiced. I mention this because choral word-by-word reading serves no useful purpose as far as I can tell.

Teacher Models Initial Pages.   Smith (1979) provided evidence that when the teacher began the reading of a text (a basal story in this case), with the students following along in their own texts, the students read the remainder of the story with

---

Shut the Book and Listen

One technique for largely eliminating interruptions when children are reading is to have everyone but the reader close the book and just listen. (The teacher and students might keep their finger in the book to mark the page for easy location after the reader completes the segment.) This technique focuses other group members' attention on how the reading sounds, as well as on whether the reading makes sense. When it does not make sense, which can only usually be determined when the reader reaches the end of a sentence, the listeners can simply prompt the reader to reread.

greater fluency and fewer misread words. This may occur because as the teacher reads the first two or three pages aloud, unique words are pronounced for the students, especially character and location names, or because the fluent reading model provides a good sense of the story line as well as a model of fluency.

Echo Reading.   In echo reading the teacher typically reads a paragraph or a page (in easier texts) aloud and then has the students chorally reread that segment. The teacher provides the fluent model, reading in phrases and with appropriate intonation. But this read aloud also introduces new words and gives the readers a sense of the story as well as the fluent model to emulate.

Whole-Class Instructional Redesign

In most of the reported research, the use of tutorial or small-group approaches to improving reading fluency has been studied. In these studies the focus was improving on the fluency and comprehension of struggling readers in particular. But there may be times when a focus on improving reading fluency might be considered useful as a whole-class intervention. The most convincing evidence on the power of a whole-class approach using repeated readings for fostering improved reading achievement comes from a study of fluency-oriented reading lessons reported by Stahl, Heubach, and Cramond (1997).

Fluency-Oriented Reading Instruction.   This was a two-year project conducted in the second grade classrooms of three elementary schools, all with diverse student populations. The intervention had three major components. First, basal reader lessons were redesigned with an emphasis on repeated readings and partner-reading to improve fluency. While fluency was emphasized, the lessons were comprehension oriented since a focus on comprehension seems to enhance fluency and vice versa. Thus, the teacher discussed the story using a story map framework after first reading the story aloud to the students. The story was then "echo read" with the whole group or with small groups of students. In echo reading the teacher read a segment and then the students reread it chorally. Next came partner reading with pairs sharing the rereading of the story. Then came a third rereading that was sometimes made into a performance activity with different students reading different characters' roles, for instance.

Second, students had home reading assignments. These involved rereading the basal story to a parent or other adult one or two days a week. Thus, the students would read and reread each basal story approximately five times to at least three different audiences (teacher, peer, parent).

Third, students engaged in daily self-selected reading. This fifteen- to thirty-minute block of time allowed children to read books from their classroom or school libraries, to reread previous basal stories or little books used instructionally, or to read books brought from home. In addition, self-selected reading was encouraged throughout the day as a "sponge" activity when children had finished other assigned work.

Over the two years of the intervention, all but two of the children who had entered second grade reading on the primer level or higher were reading on or above grade level at the end of the year. Yearly gains averaged 1.8 grade equivalents, or almost twice the expected gain and more than twice the historical gains of second graders in these schools. Half the students who entered second grade unable to read even primer-level materials were reading on grade level by the end of the year. The largest gains in achievement were made by students who entered second-grade reading below grade level.

One final comment about this study must be made. This intervention was implemented within the constraints of district mandated basal reader instruction, including in some sites, mandated-whole-class lessons from a single basal. Such is the real world. But the interesting thing about the findings was that the repeated reading and comprehension support seemed to help make the basal texts more appropriate, in the sense of difficulty, for the lower-achieving readers. Stahl and his colleagues comment that often on the initial reading of a basal story the lower achieving children's accuracy fell below the instructional level standards. But with the support provided by the several rereadings and comprehension emphasis, their accuracy improved with each rereading.

Obviously, many students made substantial gains even though the texts would seem more difficult than is usually recommended. However, the level of support provided, as well as the opportunity for repeated readings, seems to allow these more difficult texts to be used profitably. Nonetheless, it seems possible that more appropriate texts might have benefited the one-half of the lowest readers who made the less impressive progress during the intervention period.

Read Naturally.   Candace Ihnot has developed a commercial training package (and supportive materials including assessment texts, timers, etc.) that she calls Read Naturally (readnat@aol.com). This intervention involves teacher modeling of fluent reading (or taped models), repeated reading of texts, and monitoring of student reading rate progress. I know of no published studies of Read Naturally that meet the REA standards but the developer reports that in one urban district students averaged an 18-percentile-rank gain each year of Reading Naturally use. In addition, they report that 45 percent of the Title I students using Read Naturally "achieved out" Title I by scoring above the 40 percentile. But these are not independent evaluations.

Shared Book Experience.   Others have also redesigned classroom lessons with a focus on repeated readings and also found positive effects. For instance, Reutzel, Hollingsworth, and Eldredge (1994) compared the shared books experience (SBE) with the oral recitation lesson in second-grade classrooms in two schools and the same researchers (Eldredge, Reutzel, & Hollingsworth, 1996) compared the effects of ten minutes of daily SBE to ten minutes of round-robin reading practice on second-grade readers' fluency, accuracy, vocabulary acquisition, and comprehension. In both studies the SBE produced statistically superior impacts on all measures of reading proficiency. In fact, the results demonstrated a substantial positive impact for SBE, especially on the reading performances of average and struggling readers.

The SBE was adapted for the reading lessons offered in many basal anthologies published in the early and mid–1990s. However, some evidence suggests that many teachers continued to use variations of the more traditional directed reading activity and many continued using round-robin reading practice (Hoffman et al., 1998). This seems an unfortunate turn of events (as is the return of some publishers to the traditional directed reading model) given the consistently positive evidence of the greater success of the SBE in developing reading fluency and comprehension. However, SBE can be implemented with many different reading materials, though most of the research has been done using predictable and patterned language texts or authentic children's literature.

In the studies noted above the SBE was implemented following the general guidelines provided by Holdaway (1979). These included beginning with a big book version of the text to be read. This big book is placed in a position where all children in the group can readily view the print (usually from their seats on the floor in a designated group reading area). The teacher then:

- leads a discussion of the title, cover art, and the illustrations;
- invites students to predict the story line;
- reads the text aloud dramatically;
- leads the response to the story, with discussion and perhaps a retelling; after which,
- the text is read and reread several times.

On subsequent rereadings the teacher often highlights word structure (letter-sounds, onset-rhyme patterns, inflections, syllables) and language patterns (repetition, rhyme, unique words) by covering words (or word parts) with sticky notes and asking students to predict and confirm. Often children reread the story in pairs or chorally read the story aloud with their teacher.

In SBE it is the teacher who largely decides just what features of texts to focus on in rereadings. In other words, the teacher responds to students, selecting text elements based on student needs as observed in their responses during and after reading. While the basal lessons provided a focus based on an analysis of the text being read, the designers could not reliably predict just which text features might need attention in different groups of children. Thus, the successful use of SBE requires that the teacher pay more attention to student responses and then adapts lessons based more on student responses than on the suggestions found in a teacher's guide that accompanies a reading series.

The results of the experiments with the SBE intervention demonstrated positive effects on the development of reading proficiency through rigorous, replicated scientific research. After four months, students in the shared book experience classrooms had better word analysis performance, better comprehension of materials read, and the fluency of both groups improved. The repeated readings of the texts as a group and the word study in the context of the stories read, along with the discussion of the stories and the focus on text features fostered the improved performances demonstrated in the classrooms using the SBE.

Repeated Readings for Interpretation.   Francine Stayter and I (1991) described one middle school classroom where repeated readings were used to help foster higher-order comprehension. In this case, students reread materials, often aloud, attempting to become fluent and experimenting with different intonation and stress. Of particular importance was an attempt to read dialogue with accuracy and intonation. In other words, how did the character utter that line? Sarcastically? Spitefully? Apologetically? Students told us how the repeated readings often opened their eyes to alternative interpretations of the text. How they "saw" new things about characters as they reread and became familiar and comfortable with the text and the character's voice.

Rereading for Performance.   In some respects what we observed is akin to what seems to happen in Readers' Theater, Be the Character, and in the Oprah activities. In each case, readers must attempt to take on the actual voice of the characters as well as attitude, stance, and personality. In each case multiple readings of the text, or segments of the text, are necessary. In the classes where Readers Theater, Be the Character, or Oprah techniques are regularly used, some restructuring has taken place if only the elimination of some more traditional follow-up activities (question answering, worksheet completion, journal writing) in order to provide time to rehearse and perform. While it is often upper-grade teachers who have accomplished such redesign of their lessons, it isn't only older readers who can benefit from these activities.

Readers' Theater.   There are two basic approaches to Readers' Theater. First is the use of commercially prepared materials, usually scripts developed from stories of scenes in children's books. Often basal reader anthologies contain at least one script that can be performed as a play.

However, I prefer a second approach, the development of short scripts from the books and stories that children are reading. My preference for the self-developed approach stems from the fact that I believe (no reliable, replicable scientific research here) that having students involved in selecting and preparing a script has its own value. First, students are more engaged because they must locate a segment that is of interest to them or that they believe portrays an important aspect of the story or book they have been reading. This, in itself, involves higher-order engagement with a story. Second, having students develop the script focuses attention on just how authors embed dialogue in stories and books. This is another useful learning experience in my view and would seem potentially productive for improving the use of dialogue in the students' own compositions.

The commercially available scripts may be useful in helping students understand the basic format of scripting, since it seems unlikely that most students will be familiar with just how scripts are structured. But after a short experience with a commercial script I suggest the use of teacher- and student-developed scripts. Begin with a jointly developed script that draws on a book or story that is familiar to students. In developing the script with students use an easy book with few characters for the model; *Frog and Toad* (Lobel) and *Three up a Tree* (Marshall) come to mind. Read the story aloud and then select a scene with a few lines of dialogue to script. Model the format and produce the script on large sheets of chart paper. The scene should not be a long scene, usually a few lines for each character is sufficient.

After the scene is scripted on the chart paper, give the students a few minutes to read through the script a couple of times. You might then do a choral reading of the script, modeling changing voices for different characters. Now ask for volunteers to read different parts. Then have the students pair up (in the case of *Frog and Toad* or triple up for *Three Up a Tree*) and practice performing the script. Finally, have different sets of students perform their rendition for everyone.

With this preparation the students should now be allowed to simply plow ahead on their own and experiment with script development from stories or books of their choice. Students might work individually, in pairs, or teams to develop scripts, practice and, ultimately, perform their scripts for others.

Be the Character.   This is typically a solo performance although I have seen duets. In Be the Character a child simply assumes the role of a character they have selected from the story or book. They prepare a short performance, often a solo dialogue developed from the book. Sometimes they even create a simple costume of one sort or another to carry the portrayal a step further.

In one fourth-grade classroom, for instance, I watched as a young man transformed himself into Augustus Gloop from *Charlie and the Chocolate Factory*, including dressing in a large blue windbreaker supplemented by a couple of pillows. He had written a brief script from the novel that simply began, "I am Augustus Gloop…" and he then summarized his various dilemmas in a two-minute performance. The performance was quite convincing even though I understood not a word since this was a dual language classroom and this young man was reading the novel in its Spanish translation and delivered his performance accordingly.

Character Masks

One neat idea I recently observed was the use of paper plates stapled to Popsicle sticks as character masks during a performance. The children had simply drawn faces that they felt represented the character on the paper plates and then stapled on the sticks as handles. As they performed they held the paper plates up in front of their faces. This technique seemed to alleviate the anxiety that some children had about performing in front of others. The ease of construction and the eagerness of the children to create and use the masks sold me on the use of such masks.

Being on Oprah.   This activity can be organized in several ways but the basic feature is the same: Children take on the role of a book character who is appearing on a talk show. In other words, they step into the role of one of the characters in the story or book they have read. The teacher often plays the role of the talk show host in announcing the guest and beginning the dialogue with a general prompt such as, "So tell me a little bit about yourself." While similar in intent to Reader's Theater, the organization of this activity is different in that students do not act out a scene but, rather, they assume a role and respond extemporaneously as if they were the character.

I have seen individual character representations. Here one student assumed the role of the key character while the teacher and other students (or a small group of students who have read the same text) engaged the character in a discussion of his or her role, actions, and feelings during one or more episodes. In other classrooms a number of students assume the roles of different characters while the teacher and the remaining students query them about their roles and responses.

For instance, in one fourth-grade classroom, a half-dozen children assumed the roles of key characters in *Charlotte's Web* (White). They were seated facing the class. The remaining children posed queries to the children representing the various characters. All children had written possible questions in their journals as they read the book. In this classroom, the students easily took

Commercial Audiotapes of Texts

You may have noticed that the use of commercial audiotape recordings of texts has not yet been recommended. The reason is that there are so few such tapes where the reading is done slowly enough for struggling readers to actually follow along. Now this may seem an odd complaint given the emphasis in this chapter on developing fluency and improving reading rate. But professional readers simply read too fast. Struggling readers cannot keep up! This first occurred to me when I observed struggling readers in listening centers just looking at the pictures as they listened to book tapes. But a little investigative work soon located the problem. No matter how they tried, even with bell tones signaling to turn the page, the kids couldn't keep up with the professional reader.

It may not be surprising, then, that little evidence indicates that such tapes enhance fluency or reading achievement. The commercial audiotapes allow children to hear stories they cannot read but they don't seem to reliably foster fluency or achievement. However, you might want to have students make book tapes for other students to listen to. This is one strategy for making rereading a purposeful activity. In other words, a student practices reading a text in order to sound good on the tape. A tape that other kids, perhaps younger children, will listen to.

on the voice and personality of the characters they were portraying. Some acted a bit snooty, others a bit shy. In another fifth-grade classroom, three students took on the roles of key characters in *Island of Blue Dolphins* (O'Dell). The young man playing the role of the dog even growled as he responded to queries from the teacher/hostess and the remaining students/audience!

The Puppet Show.   Finally, puppet shows also provide an alternative performance activity to foster fluency and interpretation. In this case, students create simple puppets, sock puppets, string puppets, stick puppets, and so on, and from behind a screen introduce a character through the puppet. In one classroom, students created a puppet representing the historical character whose biography they had read. They prepared a three-minute performance taking the role of the character and presenting a first-person narrative they had composed.

SUMMARY

Fluent reading is an important milestone in reading development. Some students struggle mightily and slowly improve their reading scores but never seem to achieve fluency. Often these are the struggling readers—always lagging behind their peers. They are often children who only read when we request them to. In other words, they rarely engage in voluntary reading, perhaps because word-by-word reading just does not provide any personal fulfillment. Perhaps they have had only the rare opportunity to read texts of an appropriate level of complexity and so comprehension has rarely been strong. Given the demonstrated links between fluency and comprehension, it isn't particularly surprising that many word-by-word readers choose not to read much. When reading generates little or no comprehension, why would anyone continue to read? Perhaps to comply with a teacher (or parent) request. But children who do not read voluntarily stand little chance of ever engaging in enough reading to become a proficient reader.

The good news is that there are a substantial number of rigorously designed research studies demonstrating (1) that fluency can be developed, most readily through a variety of techniques that involve rereading texts and (2) that fostering fluency has reliable positive impacts on comprehension performance. Thus, when fluency is an instructional goal, and it should be for struggling readers, we have a wealth of research to guide our instructional planning. Fluency training, when focused on self-monitoring, fosters the development of a basic strategy that all readers must acquire but there are other important proficiencies that fluent reading seems necessary for.

For instance, fluency seems important in the development of the higher-order literacy proficiencies. This is because engaging in these sorts of thinking about texts, ideas, characters, and themes would seem to require substantial mental activity space. Such demonstrations of higher-order literacy proficiencies would seem more likely if the material was read accurately, fluently, and with reasonable recall of text content. In such situations, the reader would have the basic building blocks of thoughtful literacy. But when a reader struggles with word-by-word reading, having difficulty reading the sentences in phrases, it isn't surprising that little in the way of higher-order literacy performance is evident. So much cognitive effort was deployed at the word and sentence level that little remained for thinking about the ideas, emotions, and images found in the text. Working to develop fluent reading is important for fostering more thoughtful literacy performances.

5

KIDS NEED TO DEVELOP THOUGHTFUL LITERACY

The new national and state standards for proficient reading target a more thoughtful literacy than has traditionally been expected of school reading programs. What I mean is that the latest assessments of reading proficiency typically include extended response items that often require (1) that students actually think about what they have just read and (2) that they explain or describe this thinking. Being asked to think about the text you've just read is different from being asked to recall the text you've just read. And quite different from being asked to simply copy information from that text into a blank on a worksheet or to match information in the text with answer stems on a multiple-choice test.

These new thoughtful literacy assessments are attempting to move closer to measurement of the proficiencies that seem to mark a person as literate. Consider how, in the world outside of school, we judge a person's "literateness." Let's say you and I both read the same news story about the direction in which the stock market is going. When completed, do we then quiz each other? Create multiple-choice tests to be answered while rereading the article? No. We talk. Actually we converse. Each of us makes judgments about the other's understanding based on the conversation. I might even ask you about a word or phrase used in the article but usually only if I know that you are more expert about the stock market than me. In other words, I don't ask questions to *test you* but to *help me*. If you are more expert you will usually answer my question. You don't tell me to guess or to go back and read the article again. Even if you aren't more expert you will try to help. In such cases, however, you and I will try together to make some sense. We will hypothesize and weigh the evidence and draw on our combined experiences as readers as well as our combined experiences with the stock market. If the issue seems personally important enough to one or both of us, we will likely try to find someone else who can help. If it is not deemed personally important we will jointly shrug our shoulders, shake our heads, and curse financial writers for their failure to write in plain English.

But the conversation could turn in a different direction. If we are both reasonably knowledgeable we may converse about the adequacy/accuracy of the article. If, for instance, the author cautions about a possibly impending market decline, we might debate whether the predictions and advice offered seem accurate. We might judge whether the cautionary advice is supported by the data in the article *and* by our own individual prior knowledge and experiences. We would not necessarily be surprised to find that we disagree wholly with each other on whether we believe that the author has accurately predicted the market's behavior. Or we could agree on the prediction but not on the value of the recommendations. One of us might accept the advice while the other rejects it, even though we both agreed that the prediction the author made was likely to be accurate.

We might revisit this conversation at some later date. Perhaps after the market prediction was fulfilled. We would again converse and even return to what the article *said*. We might even conclude that one of us had acted more appropriately on the prediction.

My point here is that our conversations about texts we've read are much more sophisticated than the usual "recitation script" (Tharp & Gallimore, 1989) found after reading in school settings. Outside of school we actually do typically converse about what we have read. In schools children have typically "recited" what they've read. Recited in the sense that the emphasis has been on "just the facts." Often very trivial facts. Known-answer questions have dominated school reading lessons, at least since researchers began classroom observations (Cuban, 1993). But known-answer questions are largely unique to school. They are not legal in out-of-school conversations.

Imagine that you are talking with a friend. Imagine that you ask a known-answer question. You ask for the location of the nearest hardware store, even though you already know the answer. Your friend replies, correctly, and you give her a sticker and say, "Good job, you've got your thinking cap on." Would your friend be pleased with your reply and the sticker? Or confused, wondering whether you've gone mad? Or whether you are just "acting like a teacher"?

Now imagine that your friend has been reading the same newspaper that you read earlier today. You sit down and construct a set of known-answer questions based on what you remember from the news story (or better yet, you go back through the article to find "sticklers" that you think your friend probably won't remember). As soon as your friend finishes reading, you begin the quiz. "What was the name of the INS official quoted in the front-page story? What model aircraft experienced problems last night at that airport in Arkansas? Which tobacco company did the lawyer quoted in the Great American Smoke Out article represent? What was the job title of the Pakistani official quoted in the article on nuclear proliferation?" And so on. Your friend will not be an eager participant in this activity.

We do not quiz friends on the newspaper articles they've read. Nor the books they've read. However, we do discuss the articles and books. We engage in conversations about the texts, typically focusing on the ideas in the texts. The gist of the article or book. We also offer our responses, reactions, and evaluations of the ideas and information offered.

Often we discuss the perspective of the writer of the text. In other words, we look for bias. In such instances we consider the status of the author. In news reports we consider the status of the informants who are quoted. If we know that the author or informant is linked to particular political or advocacy groups (e.g., Democratic party, Christian Coalition, Greenpeace) it makes a difference in how we view the information and ideas offered. If we know the age, gender, ethnicity, or religion of the author or informant it may affect how we weigh the information. If we know the informant is likely to profit financially (or professionally) if her advice is accepted we may take this into account. In other words, we constantly monitor an author's or informant's perspective as we imagine it.

When we discuss books that we've read outside of school, we focus on our response to the book. We actively promote some texts (You have to read this… This was a wonderful book…). We pan others (Don't waste your time…). We talk comparatively about the book (I liked her other books better… This book is better than…). When our conversational partner has also read the book we may focus, positively or negatively, on certain aspects of the book (Wasn't his description of the savageness of the poverty in Dublin chilling? What did you think of her depiction of teachers?). Often our judgments about the adequacy of an author's portrayal of people, events, or situations draw heavily upon our own experiences.

When you consider the richness of the talk about texts that occurs outside of school, the typical patterns of school talk about texts seem shallow and barren. Outside school we rely on the richness of a person's conversation about texts to judge how well they understood it. Their literateness. In school we typically rely on the flat recitation of events or information to make that same judgment. Outside of school settings we engage in conversations about the adequacy of texts and authors to inform, engage, and entertain us. In school we engage in interrogations around what was "in the text."

CONVERSATION AND CONNECTIONS

I hope the discussion above helps make the enormous differences between school interactions around texts and normal out-of-school interactions a bit clearer. My main point is that school literacy interactions have often been very different from real-world literacy interactions. One key difference is that outside of school we make a variety of text-to-self, text-to-texts, and text-to-world connections when we converse about shared texts (Keene & Zimmerman, 1997). Let me try to develop each of these connections a bit more thoroughly.

Making Connections

Text-to-self connections occur when, after reading the financial news article, we say things like, "I'm worried. I need the money I have invested for tuition." Or, "I lost a bunch of money the last time the market fell, so I am worried it might happen again." After reading a novel in which a divorce figures centrally, we might say, "I felt the same way." Or, "My sister's divorce was not nearly so unpleasant." In other words, as we read we make connections between personal experiences and the text—even with informational texts. When we talk about what we've read the text-to-self connections just naturally appear.

Text-to-text connections occur when we discuss other texts in relation to the text just read. For instance, as part of the financial article discussion we might allude to other texts we've read on the topic. We might say, "There was a *Wall Street Journal* article on this topic that offered a clearer explanation." Or, "There was a *Money* magazine article this month that used the same data but came to a different conclusion." And then add a text-to-self connection, "I'm going to play it safe though and move my money out of the stock market." When reading a novel we might also make a text-to-text connection. "This book just reminded me so much of Sue Grafton's work." Or, "This character is so similar to Officer Jim Chee in the Hillerman books."

Finally, in text-to-world connections we link what we've read to what we already know about the world. This "world knowledge" may have come from daily observations, reading, listening, watching television, travel, and so on. Most often, our world knowledge is an amalgamation of the information and experiences we've accumulated over time. We may know, for instance, that palm trees grow only in mild climates. We may also know why. Or not. How we know this is typically hard to discern precisely. We may have noticed palm trees when we visited mild climates. We may have seen palm trees in movies or TV shows set in mild climates. We may have read illustrated books where palm trees appeared in the pictures when the setting was in a mild climate. Of course, if we have lived in Minnesota or Vermont or Finland we also noticed that no palm trees grew in these environments. But few of us have ever taken a course on palm trees or even read a book about palm trees. Nonetheless, when we pick up a magazine with a photo of a location that includes a palm tree we infer the mild climate. When we read about "sitting under the palms on the beach" we infer a particular geographic setting—a geographical band where the story might take place. In other words, we make text-to-world connections to help us puzzle through life and literacy.

Similarly, we would be skeptical, to put it mildly, of a history text that had General George Washington arriving at Valley Forge in a Range Rover. Or depicting President John F. Kennedy as a devout Southern Baptist. Or as a conservative Republican. Rarely could we pinpoint the exact source of our world knowledge in these instances. In other words, I "just know" Kennedy was Catholic and Democrat. I could tell you how to verify this information but I could not tell just how I came to "know" this. At least not by identifying the specific sources that provided me with that information. Nonetheless, as I read I cannot suppress my world knowledge. It is always back there, fostering a constant comparison of what I'm reading to what I "know."

When literate people talk about the texts they've read outside of school their talk is laced with connections they have made. It is these connections that drive the conversation.

Demonstrations of thoughtful literacy seem to require that the reader be able to talk in certain ways that go beyond simply making connections, though. Literate talk about texts also involves summarizing, synthesizing, analyzing, and evaluating the ideas in the text.

Summarizing.   We are constantly called on to summarize texts outside of school. If I ask you, "Did you read the article about whole language in today's paper?" You may respond, "No, what did it say?" Typically what you want to know is the gist of the article. Was it positive or negative? If negative (or positive) what evidence or examples were presented? What else you want to know will depend a lot on other factors such as your occupation (first-grade teachers might be more interested than stock brokers, for instance), or your experiences (you have a child enrolled in a school where that philosophy dominates). Regardless, you most often do not expect a full recounting of all of the details. If the topic is of great personal interest you may go find the paper or magazine and read the piece yourself.

Now summary is actually a bit more complicated than this. When you summarize you may also include references to your own experiences (text-to-self) or other things that you have read (text-to-text). In fact, your experiences and your familiarity with the topic have an enormous impact on your summary (Gaskins, 1996). In other words, you might begin summarizing the article on whole language by saying, "It's another one of those teacher-bashing articles that the *Post* is famous for." Someone else, with different experiences, might begin by saying, "The *Post* hit the nail on the head again about teachers and that social promotion nonsense." In fact, one of the skills we develop as listeners and readers is the ability to analyze a speaker's perspective or stance on an issue. Summary is rarely a "Just the facts" retelling in real world exchanges outside school.

Analyze.   When we read a text outside school we typically engage in various forms of analysis. For instance, we evaluate plot lines in novels—too outrageous, believable, imagined. We analyze the assertions in an informational text—accurate, supported, reasonable. Often, again, these analyses are connected to other experiences. We make text-to-world comparisons when we reject the premise that the hero could survive for four months with no food and water. Or that he survived on coconuts in the arctic. We engage in text-to-text connections when we note the similarity of a plot line to that of one in another book. Or when we notice that the newspaper article on wealth omits data we recently read in *Time* about the rising numbers of children living in poverty. We reject an author's claim that nicotine is not addictive with a text-to-self analysis based on our own experiences with smoking and quitting—or attempting to. In fact, often our analyses involve both summary and synthesis.

Synthesize.   Synthesis is the combining of multiple sources of information in a coherent fashion. But synthesis literally requires that we have summarized the key elements of what we've previously read. And synthesis typically requires some analysis. For instance, synthesis typically requires that we make judgments about the relative accuracy of information in various sources. We might analyze information on the importance of children's preschool experiences across a number of texts looking for data that supported or undermined the assertions made in an article that made light of such experiences in predicting school success.

But many of these analyses would be rooted in text-to-self, text-to-text, and text-to-world comparisons. Ultimately, though, we have to try and pull all the information judged relevant together into the coherent whole we call synthesis. In doing this we go beyond just providing a summary of summaries.

Evaluate.   Finally, we also routinely offer our evaluation of the texts we've read. As we talk with a colleague about an article on whole language or school vouchers we may characterize the piece as "malicious," "right-wing," "scary," or even "rambling." When we read novels we evaluate them on engagingness, pace, length, and, maybe, on literary qualities.

Suffice it to say, outside of school we talk about the things we've read in complex and varied ways. Interestingly, some kids talk that way about the texts they've read also—outside of school. But too often in school talk about the texts that have been read reflects few of the dimensions of complexity found in the out-of-school talk about texts. Too often the in-school talk seems unlikely to foster much thoughtful literacy of the sort that literate adults demonstrate every day. At the same time, the new standards and the new assessments all point to developing a more thoughtful literacy in all students.

I think it is time for us to begin rethinking the nature of this thing we've called comprehension. I think it is time we reorganized school lessons so that thoughtful literacy proficiencies are developed in all students, especially the struggling readers.

Isn't Thoughtful Literacy Just a Buzz-Word for Comprehension?

The school tasks we have traditionally labeled as comprehension tasks have been largely focused on remembering, a very narrow slice of what is needed for understanding what we read. The two types of tasks—remembering and understanding tasks—are linked at some level. I mean if you couldn't remember anything about a text that you'd read it would be impossible to demonstrate any sort of understanding. Or engage in any intelligent conversation about that text. At the same time, we can remember that a newspaper article reported that the Dow-Jones Industrial Average (DJIA) fell by 150 points, but have no real sense of what that might mean. Nor any understanding of how the DJIA is calculated. Or what companies comprise the DJIA. Or even whether the drop has any impact on our retirement investments. We could memorize the companies that are included in the DJIA and still be no closer to understanding the information in the article.

Likewise, we might remember characters, setting, and the basic plot of a moral tale without understanding the moral message. We might remember facts about the Battle of Gettysburg or the process of photosynthesis and yet have no real understanding of the importance of either. We might remember the words to the Pledge of Allegiance with no understanding of what they meant. But a thoughtfully literate conversation about any of these topics would involve a demonstration of various sorts of understanding. Quizzing each other on the details of the Battle of Gettysburg would be an unlikely out-of-school activity (except on *Jeopardy* and *Millionaire*). Discussing, that is; sharing information, experiences, and understandings about the horror of Gettysburg and its strategic role in the War of Northern Aggression would not only be a more typical event but also a more obviously thoughtful one. (Note to all readers who have spent their lives living above the Mason-Dixon Line: What some folks call the Civil War is, or was, called the War of Northern Aggression by others, usually those who lived lives below the Mason-Dixon Line.)

My point is that in school we have, in my mind, too often confused remembering with understanding. We have focused on recitation of texts, not thoughtful consideration and discussion of texts. There are times that I think our emphasis on remembering actually impedes children's understanding and the development of thoughtful literacy proficiencies. Think back to the example of the news story questions offered above.

It is entirely possible for us to understand a story without remembering all of the details. We may not remember the official title of a person who is quoted but that will not necessarily detract from understanding what he or she said. We may not be able to recall Officer Jim Chee's name but we can describe him in detail including information about his heritage, occupation, matrimonial status, personality, and so on. In other words, we could discuss him as a character—likable, dogged, spiritual, and so on. All without being able to remember his name.

Now when we begin to discuss such things we are entering the arena called thoughtful literacy. In other words, we are going beyond remembering and through the discussion we demonstrate our thinking about Officer Chee. Or about airline safety. Or the stock market. In demonstrating our thinking we demonstrate our understanding.

To me, then, thoughtful literacy represents something different from the narrow, remembering-focused tasks that have dominated school comprehension lessons. Thoughtful literacy goes beyond the ability to read, remember, and recite on demand. Generally speaking, American students are better able to demonstrate proficiency on those sorts of tasks than on thoughtful literacy tasks (Brown, 1991; Donahue et al., 1999). But if we focus children's attention almost exclusively on remembering after reading, I worry that they will confuse recall with understanding. And if we fail to provide students with models and demonstrations of thoughtful literacy and lessons on how to develop those proficiencies I fear that we will continue to develop students who don't even know that thoughtful literacy is the reason for reading (Wilhelm, 1997).

School and Thoughtful Literacy

Much of my research career has been devoted to simple demonstrations of the commonsense notion that children are most likely to learn what they are taught. In other words, if we observe the nature of the work that children and adolescents do during the school day, we can predict what sorts of skills, attitudes, habits, and knowledge they will be most likely to acquire (Doyle, 1983;

Goodlad, 1983; Bruer, 1994). If school comprehension tasks are primarily remembering tasks, then we should expect that students will get better at remembering. They are more likely to develop skills and habits that foster remembering in environments that emphasize remembering.

If few school tasks require students to think, to demonstrate that they actually understand what they have read, then it is unlikely that most will demonstrate the sorts of thinking and understanding that seem central to thoughtful literacy and attainment of the new literacy standards. When students have few opportunities to summarize, analyze, synthesize, and discuss what they've read, we should not be surprised that they demonstrate little proficiency with such tasks. When they have not only few such opportunities but have also experienced little instruction focused on fostering thoughtful literacy we should expect that rather few students will develop thoughtful literacy.

The research on the nature of school tasks suggests the reason that few American students seem thoughtfully literate. In study after study (Allington et al., 1996; Dahl & Freppon, 1995; Elmore, Peterson, & McCarthy, 1996; Goodlad, 1983; Hoffman et al., 1998; Johnston et al., 1999; Knapp, 1995; Pressley et al., 2000; Turner, 1995) researchers report that in the typical classroom the assigned tasks overwhelmingly emphasize copying, remembering, and reciting with few tasks assigned that engage students in thinking about what they've read.

The situation for struggling readers seems even more dire. Researchers have consistently reported that lower-achieving readers spent little of their school day on comprehension tasks of any sort. Struggling readers simply read less often in their classrooms, which limited the availability of comprehension tasks. Instead, for these students the lesson focus was often on words, letters, and sounds (Allington, 1983; Collins, 1986; Hiebert, 1983; Ysseldyke et al., 1984). It is tough to do much comprehension work with phonics worksheets or drill or with flashcards or contractions dittoes. Worse, the same patterns were found in studies that examined the nature of the lessons offered these students in their remedial reading and learning disabilities classes (Allington & McGill-Franzen, 1989; Jenkins et al., 1988; Johnston & Allington, 1991; McGill-Franzen & Allington, 1990; Thurlow et al., 1984; Zigmond, Vallecorsa & Leinhardt, 1980).

The demonstrated failures of the skills-emphasis instructional programs—in general, remedial and special education programs—to foster improved reading generally and improved comprehension especially (Carter, 1984; Glass, 1983; Leinhart & Pallay, 1982; Venezky, 1998) has stimulated substantial interest in rethinking the nature of reading instruction. Curriculum focused on promoting more thoughtful lessons produced not only better comprehension achievement but also equal or better skills achievement than the curriculum that emphasized mastery of isolated skills (Dole, Brown & Trathen, 1996; Knapp, 1995; Pressley, 1990; Purcell-Gates, McIntyre & Freppon, 1995).

Thus, the disappointment with the effectiveness of the skills-mastery curriculum has generated much experimentation in American classrooms and stimulated a wealth of classroom-based studies of thoughtful literacy. Whether the research was of a more naturalistic design or more experimental in nature, the evidence converges on two key findings: the research available indicates that (1) classrooms do differ on this dimension and (2) the differences matter in terms of the skills, attitudes, habits, and knowledge that students acquire.

THE EFFECTS OF THOUGHTFUL LITERACY INSTRUCTION

Researchers have used a variety of methods in studying thoughtful literacy, in part because different research teams had different research questions. Some were interested in studying how aspects of thoughtful literacy instruction emerged in classrooms (Allington et al., 1996; Duffy, 1993; Elmore et al., 1996; Johnston et al., 1998; Langer, 1995; Scharer, 1992). In these studies it was commonly reported that creating thoughtful classrooms was often difficult. Thoughtful literacy lessons seem to require a different organization of instructional time and a different sort of curriculum design than those found in most schools. Thoughtful literacy lessons needed larger blocks of uninterrupted time than many schools made available to classroom teachers. Discussion and collaborative work came off easier when tables, rather than desks, were available. It required different materials; single copies of multiple texts rather than multiple copies of single texts. But most of all, thoughtful literacy lessons required teachers to think about teaching and learning differently. It required teachers to take professional risks and teach differently. Organizational support was necessary for the teacher learning, experimenting, and the risk-taking that was required.

Others studied the effects of introducing aspects of such instruction into classroom lessons on student achievement (Anderson & Roit, 1993; Beck et al., 1997; Block, 1993; Dole et al., 1996; Duffy et al., 1986; Palincsar & Brown, 1984; Pressley et al., 1992). The common finding was unsurprising in retrospect: More thoughtful lessons produced more thoughtful readers. This enhanced thoughtfulness was demonstrated on standardized tests of comprehension (typically not very sensitive to thoughtful literacy), through student writing, and on experimenter-devised assessments of problem-solving and text processing.

And others investigated outcomes beyond those assessed on standardized tests. For example, Turner (1995) reported that students in classrooms that emphasized thoughtful literacy work were more skilled in peer collaboration, took more personal responsibility for their work, and demonstrated higher levels of engagement in academic work. Knapp (1995) reported that students enrolled in thoughtful literacy classrooms were better at problem-solving, informational text comprehension, and writing. Dahl and Freppon (1995) noted persistence when confronted with difficulty was more common among students in thoughtful literacy environments while the students in the skills-emphasis classrooms demonstrated greater passivity. Hoffman et al. (1998) found that student motivation, independence, and persistence were reported by teachers as among the more common outcomes in their study of a shift to more thoughtful curriculum materials and tasks. Finally, Donahue et al. (1999) reported on the NAEP survey data that demonstrated that students who were more often asked to explain, discuss, or write about the texts they had read were also more likely to demonstrate the higher-order, thoughtful literacy proficiencies than students who had fewer such opportunities.

Thoughtful Literacy and Exemplary Teachers.   Thoughtful literacy lessons were also characteristic of the classroom instruction offered by exemplary teachers (Allington & Johnston, 2000; Brandt, 1986; Nystrand et al., 1997; Pressley et al., 2000; Ruddell, Draheim & Barnes, 1990; Taylor et al., 2000). In these studies exemplary teachers routinely produced superior achievement on standardized tests and the other evidence gathered indicates their students not only read and write more but also read and write differently from students in more typical classrooms. In these classrooms, teachers and students were more likely to make connections across texts and across conversations. The talk was more often of a problem-solving nature. In addition, the students in the exemplary teacher classrooms were more likely to be engaged in peer conversations about texts they had read. Thus, the quality and quantity of classroom talk also differed.

Summary.   Thoughtful literacy can be fostered but the classrooms most successful in developing such proficiencies look different from traditional classrooms. Nonetheless, if we want students to develop the thinking around reading and writing activity that marks thoughtful literacy, classroom instruction will necessarily change.

RESEARCH ON EFFECTIVE COMPREHENSION INSTRUCTION

There have been several major reviews of the research on the development of enhanced comprehension skills. However, much of this research has focused on how to help students perform traditional classroom comprehension tasks more adeptly. That is, how to help students prepare better for recitation tasks, primarily. But since recitation tasks seem a mainstay of schooling, and have been a core school activity for centuries, we must also consider what we have learned about how to foster improved recitation performance.

The comprehensive reviews provided by Pressley and his colleagues (1990), Dole and hers (1996), Pearson and Dole (1987), Pearson and Fielding (1991), Rosenshine and Meister (1994), and Mastroprieri and Scruggs (1997) converge on several conclusions. First, and most important, they point to strong evidence that reading comprehension performance, measured in a variety of ways, can be significantly improved with effective teaching. This is an important point because some folks have assumed, incorrectly, that reading comprehension was largely related to that thing we call intelligence. In other words, that reading comprehension "just happened" if the reader pronounced the words correctly.

What these reviews of the research demonstrate is that reading comprehension, even recitation, involves active thinking. This thinking can be improved when students are provided explicit demonstrations of the strategies that literate people use when they read—in this case, when they read school texts for school tasks.

A second conclusion from the research was that teachers could learn to provide effective instruction in strategy development but this required moving away from traditional notions of how to foster comprehension and away from heavy reliance on the teacher guides that accompanied the textbooks that were frequently used in classrooms. In other words, most "lessons" offered in the teacher guides in readers, social studies, and science texts were designed more *to assess* student recitation proficiency than *to improve* that proficiency. The lessons focused more on immediate recall of the information than on the development of transferable strategies that promoted independent use of effective thinking while reading. The teacher guides were chock full of activities but most would only provide the teacher with information on who was able to recall information bits from the story being read.

For instance, teacher guides were filled with questions to ask students—questions for oral interrogation, written end-of-chapter questions, worksheets and graphic organizers to be completed, and so on. In fact, one recent analysis reported that the number of "mindless, useless activities" was staggering. Crossword puzzles, hidden word searches, vocabulary definition tasks, all frequently accompanied the steady stream of questions offered for students to answer. But all these tasks simply assessed whether or not students could adequately respond. Rarely was there any instructional component unless individual "discovery" learning was counted as instruction.

It wasn't just the teacher guides that accompany textbooks that reflected this lack of instruction; some of the most popularly used materials and activities offered no instructional component either. For instance, neither the *Accelerated Reader* program nor the *Barnell-Loft* comprehension materials (Find the Main Idea, levels A, B, C...) provide anything but activities that assess student strategy use. I call these "assign and assess" materials because no instruction is provided. Unfortunately, the textbook teacher guides and many popular comprehension curriculum materials rely on the student acquiring useful strategies through self-discovery. But many students seem not to "discover" these strategies without teacher demonstration.

A third conclusion from the research was that strategy learning took time. The most successful interventions tapped a single strategy and developed that strategy through longer-term instruction and repeated application activity. While the traditional "main idea" lesson in a teacher guide, for instance, might last one day or, in some cases, for one week, effective strategy teaching often offered four to ten weeks of focused instruction and application of a single strategy. While the teacher guide lesson focused on a definition (A main idea is an important idea.), the effective strategy instruction focused on the thinking that students needed to apply while reading (Summarizing involves two key strategies: selecting important ideas and deleting trivial, redundant, and unrelated ideas.)

Finally, the lesson design in teacher guides moved quickly from definition to assessment and most of the suggested activities were assessments as opposed to instructional activities (questions about main idea, worksheets requiring identification of main idea, graphic organizers to be completed, etc.). The effective strategy lessons immersed students in teacher demonstrations of the thinking, the strategy-in-use, and the application of the strategy repeatedly across a number of different texts. After the four- to ten-week focus on effective strategy use, substantial improvements in comprehension were typically demonstrated. The greatest improvements were often found among the lower-achieving students.

A third conclusion from the research was that there were only a handful of strategies that seemed apparently central to improved school comprehension performance. Remember, though, that these were the strategies that (1) had demonstrated value in multiple research studies and (2) improved performance on traditional school comprehension tasks. In other words, some of the strategies may be of more use when lower-level comprehension, recitation, for instance, is the goal, than when higher-order comprehension, thoughtful literacy, is the desired result. But also remember that thoughtful literacy requires at least some recall of the text, though not necessarily the ability to recite all of the details. In my view the research summaries provide enormously useful guidelines for initiating instruction that leads to the development of thoughtful literacy. At the same time, I feel the research studies summarized in these reviews typically emphasized improved recitation, a necessary, perhaps, but still low-level indication of understanding of texts read.

Summary.   The research on comprehension strategy teaching provides powerful evidence that most struggling readers (and many not so struggling readers) benefit enormously when we can construct lessons that help make the comprehension processes visible. Many students only develop the strategies they need with much instructional support. Traditional "assign and assess" lessons (Read the chapter and answer the questions at the end.) offer little useful assistance for these students. Instead of assign and assess lessons these students need demonstrations of effective strategy use and lots of opportunities to apply the demonstrated strategy over time.

CRAFTING OPPORTUNITIES THAT ENHANCE STUDENTS' COMPREHENSION AND UNDERSTANDING

The research points to the power of particular types of instructional environments in fostering the development of thoughtful literacy, especially in struggling readers. In this section I will sketch some of the powerful instructional activities that I believe should be available in every classroom. There are two broad emphases discussed: Promoting comprehension on traditional school tasks and promoting thoughtful literacy. This is my arbitrary division and not one that is absolutely essential, I suppose. Nonetheless, I think the evidence available suggests that lessons that foster improved recitation and lessons that foster thoughtful literacy, while sharing some commonalities, differ in substantive ways. It seems to me that the most effective instruction offers both types of lessons.

Comprehension in Traditional School Tasks.   Perhaps the very first proficiency we expect children to develop (or arrive with it already developed in first grade) is summarization. At first this may be expected only after students have

Activating prior knowledge. It is important that students develop the habit of reflecting on what they already know about a text or the topic of a text before they begin reading. In classroom practice activating prior knowledge is often linked to developing predictions about the text content before reading.

Summarizing. This is, perhaps, the most common and most necessary strategy. It requires that the student provide a general recitation of the key text content. Literate people summarize informational texts routinely in their conversations. They summarize weather reports, news articles, stock market information and editorials. In each case they select certain features and delete, or ignore, other features of the texts read when they summarize.

Story grammar lessons. The use of a story grammar framework (setting, characters, problem, attempts at problem resolution, and resolution) is one of the most commonly researched instructional techniques. The goal of story grammar lessons is helping students to develop adequate summaries of narrative texts. "Adequate" is defined largely as a recitation of the key elements of the story—the story grammar elements listed above.

Imagery. Two broad types of imagery strategies have been studied. First, fostering an internal visual image of aspects of the setting, characters, and events offered in a text. The lessons were designed to help students create a visual image of what a character looked like (tall, blond, agile, twenty-something) or of a setting (a prairie sod house or the floor plan of the heroine's apartment). The second sort of imagery strategies were helping students manufacture a distinct mnemonic image to facilitate recall (imagining your friend Dan on an inner tube floating by Budapest (Dan in tube) to remember Danube as the name of the river).

Question generating. This research had students develop questions about the text as they read. There have been a number of twists on this technique ranging from developing "teacherly" questions (What question might your teacher ask about the information in this paragraph?), to author-purpose questions (What was the author trying to convince you to believe?), to text adequacy questions (What else should the author have explained if he wanted you to understand this chapter?).

Thinking aloud. These studies sometimes focused on having the teacher "think aloud" as a technique for demonstrating the thinking strategies good

(continued)

Figure 5.1
Useful Research-Based Comprehension Strategies

readers use (After reading a particular sentence aloud to students the teacher might say, "As I read this sentence I thought to myself, this doesn't make any sense because...") and at other times on the effect of having students think aloud as they read. A key aspect of this technique seems to be the intent to promote in students the sort of internal dialogue that good readers use as they read. That is, as you read this text you "think to yourself" about what you are reading. You make connections to other things you've read and to your own experiences as a reader and as a student and, perhaps, as a teacher. (Perhaps right now you are thinking, "Yeah, I agree with Allington on that. I do think to myself as I read." Or, "Is he crazy? I don't think to myself, I just try to remember what he writes for the test.") However, often the use of the think-aloud techniques was linked to developing other strategies (The teacher says, "When I read a story I pay attention to the setting...").

Figure 5.1 *continued*

listened to a story read aloud to them. "What was the story about?" is the sort of query that signals the expectation that a heard or read story will be summa-rized. In the past two decades there has been much research on the successful use of story maps as an instructional strategy (Pearson & Dole, 1987; Pressley et al., 1990). However, much of this research was conducted using older chil-dren and using a graphic organizer. Simply put, summarizing a story for school, typically has meant recalling specific story elements: setting (Long ago and faraway), key characters (A prince and a maiden), problem confronted (The Prince is under a spell), attempts at problem resolution (The maiden kisses the sleeping Prince), and resolution (They lived happily ever after). These elements were often outlined in a graphic on which children were expected to fill in the details. Instruction of the specific elements, usually with the teacher walking the children through a story and providing a model of how one would identify each element, was typically offered. The research indicated that such lessons fostered story-summarizing proficiencies.

   In one of the exemplary classrooms I have been privileged to observe, I saw a first grade teacher use the same general format to introduce her students to the story summary process. But in this case, the teacher began the instruction during the first weeks of school—before the children could read or write much. Thus, she began with a read-aloud of *Stellaluna*. After reading that text aloud several times over several days, she gathered the students at the story carpet and told them, "Today we are going to learn how to tell someone else what a book is all about. In school there are certain things people expect to hear when they ask you, 'What was the book about?' What people expect in school is that you will tell them where the story took place, who was in the story, what the problem was, and how the problem was solved. We are going to use the book, *Stellaluna*, that I've been reading to you."

She then began again reading *Stellaluna* aloud, stopping after a couple of pages. Now she noted, "Well, we know that Stellaluna is one important character in the book. So who are the other characters in this story? Who else is important in this story?" The students responded with names of the characters. She then asked, "Let's look at the pictures again from the beginning. Where does this story take place?" Students offered several answers including, "In the trees... In a forest... In the woods." "In a forest. I like that one. We'll have to remember that the story takes place in a forest with lots of trees." The teacher continued reading. After awhile she again stops and asks the students, "Stellaluna has lost her mother. I think that is the problem in this story. Do all of you agree? Would it be a problem if you lost your mother and didn't know where to find her?" Children chime in with various sorts of assenting commenting. The reading aloud then continues to the end of the book. At this point the teacher says, "Goodness, I am glad that Stellaluna solved the problem and found her mother. How about you?"

Now the teacher reviews the story summary points again. She then assigns one story element to children who sit at each of the four tables in the room. One table is to draw a picture of the important characters and copy their names from the book. Another is to draw a picture of the forest and label it. Another is assigned to illustrate Stellaluna without her mother and label the illustration. The final group is to draw a picture of Stellaluna and her mother reunited at the end of the story. The children proceed quickly to the tasks. The teacher moved about from table to table offering advice, usually on the labeling, usually having students return to the text to locate the words they wanted to use.

After a few minutes the teacher regathered the group at the story carpet asking one person at each table to bring along the illustration. She then directed the students' attention to a large piece of butcher block paper she had taped to the wall next to the story carpet area. In the center was a photocopy of the book jacket for *Stellaluna*. Now she called on one child in each group to display and explain their illustration and read their caption. Then she taped these up on the butcher paper poster: character illustration in the upper left, setting in the upper right, problem in the lower right, resolution in the lower left. And she read the book again, this time pointing to the captioned illustrations as she read the relevant sections.

Finally (though only about 20 minutes have passed since she began the first read-aloud of the day), she reminds the students that in school people expect that we will tell about a book in a certain way. She says, "I am going to use the chart we just made to help me remember how to tell someone what the book, *Stellaluna*, is all about. So, (pointing to the illustration of key characters) I would begin by saying that this is a story about a bat named Stellaluna, her mother, an owl, and some birds. Then I would say that the story (pointing to the illustration of the forest) takes place in a forest. I would say that the problem was that Stellaluna lost her mother (pointing to that illustration) but that with

This quilt-sized pictorial story map for the book, *Stelluna*, was a critical component in developing students' understandings of just how a "school retelling" is expected to go.

the help of the owl and birds she found her mother (pointing to that illustration) and was very happy again. Now let's all use the chart to tell about the book."

At this point the teacher pointed to each illustration in sequence and prompted by saying, "This is a story about…, It takes place in a…, The problem was…, But in the end…" Throughout this the children chimed in with the relevant information. On completion the teacher congratulated the students and promised they would return to the chart again.

Over the next few days the teacher reread *Stellaluna* several times and used the chart as a story summary prompt or scaffold. With each rereading and retelling she offered less advice and expected the students to provide more of the information. The following week, she read another book (*Make Way for Ducklings*) and with the children developed another chart. Again she reread and they retold the story using the chart as their prompt or scaffolding. A third book was presented in the same manner. On the fourth book, the teacher read it aloud but had individual children create their own story chart on a large piece of manila art paper. Again, the placement of the story elements remained the same, starting in the upper left and ending at the lower right. As she began this new activity she again walked the children through the story and the elements before they were expected to write or draw. Six weeks after this activity had begun, students were creating charts largely by themselves. The teacher moved from child to child and asked them to tell her what the book was all about. Mimicking the teacher's hand movements the students pointed to each captioned illustration as they retold the story. After about 10 weeks, the teacher had the students create the charts in their journals. By mid-year she had students creating story charts in their journals for books they had read independently, books they especially liked and wanted to remember. By the end of the year students were sketching story charts as a precursor to writing journal summaries of books they read.

I have taken a bit of time to develop this activity because it illustrates several essential aspects of effective strategy instruction. First, the teacher provided enormous support initially. Second, she created collaborative activities and activities where children had to verbalize their thinking. Third, she provided a sustained engagement with the summarizing activity. Fourth, she gradually moved students to greater and greater independence in using the strategy. Finally, by year's end all students could produce story summaries of the books they had read and books that were read to them.

This classroom was populated by children from lower-income homes. Many had performed dreadfully poorly on end-of-year kindergarten testing. Many seemed to have had few book and print experiences before they came to school and, unfortunately, too many had had few such experiences in a kindergarten program that focused on a "letter-of-the-week" curriculum plan with lots of worksheets and letter-naming drills but few story or book experiences.

The children in this classroom also represented a variety of ethnic groups and cultural traditions. The teacher seemed to know that not all cultures value the same type of story summary (Au, 1980; Cazden, 1988; Delpit, 1995). Nevertheless, there is only one way to retell a story in school. That way is well represented by the story elements strategy. It is a "just the key facts" retelling with "key" defined by the several story elements. Children who arrive at school (or first grade) with few experiences with books have had few opportunities to acquire story summary proficiencies. Children who arrive in first grade with little experience with the "school way" of summarizing stories are at a disadvantage. They remain disadvantaged unless we create classrooms that level the field by providing useful and explicit strategy instruction that develops the needed proficiencies. This classroom provides such powerful instruction. The performances of the children illustrated just how useful such instruction can be.

But it isn't just story, or narrative, summary that is important. Many students need similar lessons for summarizing informational texts and other types of reading materials. There are wonderful resources available for planning such lessons. And, of course, there are proficiencies beyond summarizing that students must develop. The key features of effective comprehension strategy teaching remain largely unchanged regardless of the strategy to be taught.

In truth, children need to learn how to employ the several important strategies almost simultaneously as they read. In other words, as stories become more complex and present new and unfamiliar settings and eras, activating

Beck et al. (1997). *Questioning the author.* International Reading Association. (www.reading.org).

Harvey & Goudvis (2000). *Strategies that work: Teaching comprehension to enhance understanding.* Stenhouse. (www.stenhouse.com).

Pressley & Woloshyn (1995). *Cognitive strategy instruction that really improves children's academic performance.* Brookline Books. (1-800-666-BOOK).

Robb (1996). *Reading strategies that work: Teaching your students to become better readers.* Scholastic. (www.scholastic.com).

Tierney et al. (2000). *Reading strategies and practices, 5th ed.* Allyn & Bacon. (www.abacon.com).

Figure 5.2
Wonderful Sources for Powerful Comprehension Strategy Lessons

prior knowledge, visualization, question generating, predicting and verifying, and thinking aloud all become useful, necessary strategies to be implemented on appropriate occasions. Bergman (1992) describes how such strategy use is supported in a third-grade classroom in one school district that has implemented well-researched strategy instruction. She makes it clear that teachers must provide, almost continually, explicit and implicit support for strategy use. The feature box below illustrates a classroom chart that is posted for students in one classroom. But strategy use isn't left to the students alone. Instead, the teacher refers to the chart when working with students, highlighting the queries and strategies they might focus on given the problem they are facing with a particular text.

Similarly, Beck and her colleagues (1997) provide extended classroom examples of the implementation of a technique they call Questioning the Author (QtA). One example illustrates how a teacher and her students puzzle through a social studies book using the general QtA queries as a guide. These queries include

Initiating queries:

- What is the author trying to say here?
- What is the author's message?
- Why is the author telling us that?

Follow-up queries:

- What does the author mean here?
- Does the author explain this clearly?
- How could the author have said things more clearly?
- What would you say instead?

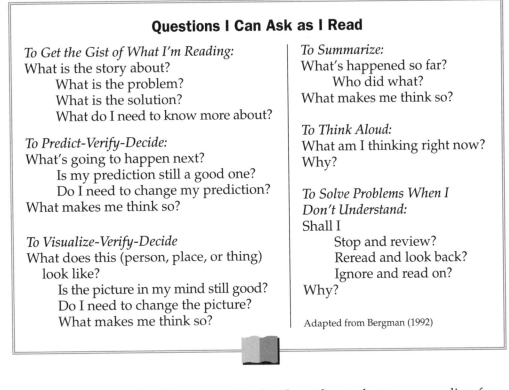

Questions I Can Ask as I Read

To Get the Gist of What I'm Reading:
What is the story about?
    What is the problem?
    What is the solution?
    What do I need to know more about?

To Predict-Verify-Decide:
What's going to happen next?
    Is my prediction still a good one?
    Do I need to change my prediction?
What makes me think so?

To Visualize-Verify-Decide
What does this (person, place, or thing)
    look like?
    Is the picture in my mind still good?
    Do I need to change the picture?
    What makes me think so?

To Summarize:
What's happened so far?
    Who did what?
What makes me think so?

To Think Aloud:
What am I thinking right now?
Why?

*To Solve Problems When I
Don't Understand:*
Shall I
    Stop and review?
    Reread and look back?
    Ignore and read on?
Why?

Adapted from Bergman (1992)

They detail a classroom episode where the students were reading from their social studies textbook and encountered this passage:

> Washington gave the Governor's letter to the French leader. No one knew this, but Washington made a drawing of the fort. Washington saw that the French planned to make war on the English. At last, the French leader gave Washington a message for the Governor. He said the French would not leave Pennsylvania.

After reading this, the teacher asks, "What is the author's message? One student replies, "That the French aren't gonna leave Pennsylvania. They just plan to keep it."

The teacher restates the comment and then asks, "What does the author say to make Quianna think that? Another student responds, "They were planning to stay, and I think that they're bound to have a war." The teacher restates the comment and then asks, "What do you think gave Dorelle that idea?" Another student replies, "Because the Governor knew that the French were staying because, um, I think he knew the French wouldn't just let the English have it without having a war." The teacher again restates the student comment and says, "I think Leah is right—there is too much at stake and there would probably be a war." Another student agrees, "They have soldiers, so why would they leave when they have soldiers there to fight?

Now that the students have understood the possibility of an impending war the teacher draws their attention to that portion of the text that tells that

Washington made a drawing of the fort. She asks, "Why do you think the author tells us this? What is the drawing of the fort all about?" A student replies, "'Cause when he gives the message to the Governor... the reason is he wants him to know what the fort looks like." The teacher again restates the student's comment and again turns the responsibility for figuring out why the Governor might want the drawing back to the students. "But why would he want to show the Governor what the fort looked like anyway?

One student responds, "Maybe because the Governor would need to know what the fort looked like, like how big it was." Another student chimes in with, "Yeah, so when he attacked, he'd know where to attack and how many soldiers and stuff he'd need to do it."

Thus, the students are led to a deeper understanding of the implicit message in this text. In fact, Beck et al. (1997) continue with their presentation of this lesson segment by noting that one student comments how often authors don't tell you everything. How often you have to figure a lot out all by yourself when you are reading. The QtA is a well-researched instructional technique that provides students with a set of useful thinking strategies to use when reading. It helps students understand that an author is attempting to communicate something and that, sometimes, authors are not very successful in their attempts.

QtA is a powerful strategy for helping struggling readers not only better understand the texts they read but also understand that some texts are just hard to understand for any number of reasons. This "blame the author" feature—she just didn't write it very clearly—can be empowering for struggling readers.

Summary.   The potential of effective strategy instruction to improve students' performance on school comprehension tasks is well documented. Unfortunately, too few classrooms routinely offer the sorts of strategy teaching that produces better comprehension. In order to enhance reading comprehension, more children need regular access to this sort of teaching. However, a caution should be heeded: Children and adolescents also need to read a lot. Do not get so taken with strategy instruction that the classroom gets out of balance in terms of time spent reading versus time spent on the other things.

Developing Thoughtful Literacy.   Thoughtful literacy is more than remembering what the text said. It is engaging the ideas in texts, challenging those ideas, reflecting on them, and so on. It is responding to a story with giggles, goosebumps, anger, or revulsion. Earlier I discussed the notion of "literate conversation"—the sort of talk around texts that literate adults routinely engage in. It is the development of this sort of proficiency that is desperately neglected in schools today. So where to begin?

Well, we could begin in kindergarten, actually. Building on her research in preschool and kindergarten classrooms McGill-Franzen (McGill-Franzen & Lanford, 1994; McGill-Franzen, 1996) examined kindergarten teachers' talk around the books they read aloud. She noted that the nature of the teacher talk not only contributed to growth in vocabulary and language knowledge but also shaped children's understandings of what it means to be literate. By helping kindergarten teachers learn to engage children in a richer talk environment during and after a story read-aloud she demonstrated the substantial impact that such shifts can have on kindergarten children's early literacy development (McGill-Franzen et al., 1999). In this case the focus was on helping kindergarten children make text-to-self and text-to-text connections as books were read across the year. While the elaborated book reading was only one feature of this kindergarten intervention, it was an important component in predicting whether the urban kindergarteners were well prepared for first grade.

One way to begin to foster literate conversation in your classroom is to consider helping students draw the text-to-self, text-to-text, and text-to-world connections (Keene & Zimmerman, 1997). You might begin by offering your own text-to-self connections with texts you read aloud to students or even with texts they are reading (even basal excerpts). For instance, if I were to read aloud (or have students themselves read) *The Barn* by Avi (Orchard Books), I would comment on my own text-to-self experiences growing up on a Midwestern dairy farm in the 1950s. While I never attended a barn raising, as in the Avi book, I could talk about how the farmers in my rural community gathered together at harvest time to assist each other. I would tell about the meals at noon under the maple trees. About making "sun tea" and cooling the jug in a fresh water spring. I would ask students about times when members of their families or their neighbors might get together to help complete a job of one sort or another. I might ask them to compose a journal entry on this link. Or to draw a picture of it and then have them describe the pictured event to a partner.

I observed one of our exemplary fourth-grade teachers make text-to-text connections as his students read a piece of historical fiction set in the era of the California gold rush. In this case he elicited a variety of connections between that text and texts read earlier ranging from the social conditions of the era to the fact that school and schooling for children was very different in that time period compared to today. Some children noted very literal connections—the role of horses as transportation, for instance—but one commented on poverty and the hope for wealth seemed a connection that linked much of the movement westward.

In another classroom the teacher connected her visit to the Gettysburg National Park with Murphy's historical book, *The Boys' War* (Clarion Books). One student connected the text to the film *Glory*, the story of the African-American Massachusetts Fifty-Fourth Regiment. This led to an amazing class discussion of how it was that children their age could be allowed to join an army. And how anyone could shoot a drummer boy even if he was "the enemy." Finally, another student connected a recent news account of child soldiers in the Far East and Africa to suggest that "boy soldiers" weren't just a terrible historical mistake. These text-to-world connections fostered much more interesting journal responses as well as greater student engagement in the texts being read and discussed.

Finally, in another classroom the teacher read Johnson's *Tell Me a Story, Mama* (Orchard Books) and then asked, "Does anyone in your family tell stories about growing up?" A dozen hands shot up as students wanted to tell

This is but a small part of a collection of books featuring the lives of children during the Civil War. The books represent several genres and a range of difficulty levels.

about Uncle Jerome or Grandma Dykstra. This led to a writing activity that involved the students describing both the relative and the stories they told. These text-to-world connections produced a number of hilarious episodes that were later shared with others at their tables and in their journals.

Similarly, Duthie (1996) describes how effective having her students develop "How to" books was in fostering not only thinking but conversation as students attempted to follow the directions their peers had written. The activity also made it clear just how difficult it is to write clear directions even for something as common as making a peanut butter sandwich or displaying appropriate manners at a wedding reception. Her lessons often focused on students' various expertise—and every student was an expert on something. Being the class expert on something allowed for all children to assume the principal role in some discussion. In other words, "Let's ask Jimmy, he's the expert on farms (or butterflies, or stomper trucks, or dinosaurs)."

Jenkins (1999) focuses on the use of one sort of text sets, in this case author studies, to foster thinking and conversation. She provides the example of students reading several books by Cynthia Rylant along with her autobiography, *But I'll Be Back Again* (Dell). Different teachers use sets of Rylant's books for dif-

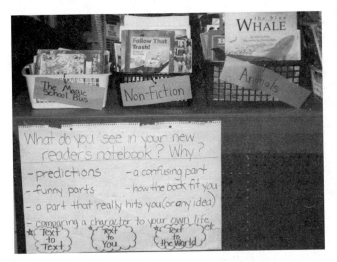

Below these various book bin collections is a poster that provides prompts for students as they write about what they've read.

ferent sorts of study but in each case the goal is the fostering of more literate conversation about the author and her books. But other sorts of text sets can also be useful tools for engaging students in text-to-text literate talk. For instance, one might use Hunts's *Across Five Aprils* and Beatty's *Turn Homeward, Hannalee,* to contrast the similarities and differences in young women of different circumstances during the Civil War. These text-to-text comparisons could be supplemented by text-to-self comparisons: How is your life different from the lives of these young women? Are there any similarities between your life and theirs?

Another technique for fostering conversation about texts is to provide students with "sticky note" pads to use as they read (Cunningham & Allington, 1999). Those ubiquitous sticky notes can be used by students to record text-to-self,

---

Wonderful Ideas for Fostering Thoughtful Literacy Can Be Found in the Texts Listed Below.

Cullinan (1993). *Children's Voices: Talk in the Classroom.* International Reading Association (www.reading.org).

Duthie (1997). *True Stories: Nonfiction Literacy in the Primary Classroom.* Stenhouse. (www.stenhouse.com).

Jenkins (2000). *The Allure of Authors.* Heinemann (www. heinemann.com).

Keene & Zimmerman (1997). *Mosaic of Thought.* Stenhouse.

Newkirk & McClure (1992). *Listening In: Children Talk about Books (and Other Things).* Heinemann.

Langer (1995). *Envisioning Literature.* Teachers College Press.

Wilhelm (1998). *You Gotta Be the Book.* Heinemann.

text-to-text, or text-to-world connections as they read. The technique requires that students are first familiar with the text-to_____connection process, perhaps after it has been introduced and practiced for a time conversationally. Once familiar, the students simply use the sticky notes to record when they make the connections while reading. I would have them use the simple abbreviations of *tt*, *ts*, and *tw* to represent the different types of connections. The thing about the sticky notes is that it allows students to "mark" the connections in their copies of the texts, which makes it easier at a later discussion group to reactivate the connections that were made.

Summary.   If we wish to help children and adolescents become thoughtfully literate, classroom talk around texts is critical. Fostering thoughtful conversation often requires a rather dramatic shift in classroom practice. But proficiency in literate conversation can be developed and, I would argue, must be. I have not mentioned the potential of activities such as Reader's Theater or other techniques that engage children in dramatic response to stories they've read but these too can assist readers in becoming thoughtfully literate.

THOUGHTFUL LITERACY AND STRUGGLING READERS

Let me close this chapter by simply noting that struggling readers have the greatest needs for lessons that foster thoughtfulness. It is these readers that too often are "flatliners" when it comes to reading. If we could elicit some sort of readout of mental activity during reading, I fear that for many struggling readers that readout would too often look like the flat EKG line so often depicted in television death scenes.

Kids need to read a lot to become proficient readers. They need books in their hands that they can read—accurately and fluently. They need books that are of interest to them. Once we have all these conditions met, we need to help all readers become more thoughtfully literate. Some will need extensive assistance in this regard, in some cases because they are exposed to little thoughtful literacy at home. These are the children who depend on the classroom lessons the most. All children benefit from good instruction—lessons that provide the sorts of demonstrations and supports that I have tried to describe in this chapter. For too long we have relied more on the assign-and-assess lessons and materials and provided too little useful strategy teaching and offered too few opportunities to engage in and develop literate talk. Changing in-school reading environments so that thoughtful literacy is fostered is one of the things that really matters for struggling readers.

6

WHERE TO BEGIN: INSTRUCTION FOR STRUGGLING READERS

I really do wish that some "quick fix"—one effectively addressing the problems of struggling readers—had been discovered. I wish someone had demonstrated the efficacy of a very low effort, inexpensive plan—a new curriculum material, a modest school day restructuring initiative, a software package. But even our best attempts have proved disappointing and our most effective attempts have been expensive. There have been demonstrations that the use of particular curricular approaches can produce very modest benefit for some struggling readers some of the time (Allington, 2001; Lyon & Moats, 1997). There have been demonstrations that restructuring the school day and reorganizing reading instruction can produce a few more children who achieve the new standards, in some schools (Allington, 1994; Slavin et al., 1996). And some day someone may demonstrate that a particular type of software can reliably produce a sustained positive effect on reading achievement, for at least some students. At this point in time, though, the best evidence available indicates that addressing the needs of struggling readers requires a comprehensive and sustained intervention effort (Allington & Walmsley, 1995). Key elements of researched-based interventions include:

- improving classroom instruction
- enhancing access to intensive, expert instruction
- expanding available instructional time
- availability across children's school careers

In the remainder of this chapter, each of these elements will be discussed.

IMPROVING CLASSROOM INSTRUCTION

The most powerful feature of schools, in terms of developing children as readers and writers, is the quality of classroom instruction. Effective schools are simply schools where there are more classrooms where high-quality reading and writing instruction is regularly available. No school with mediocre classroom instruction ever became effective just by adding a high-quality remedial

The Impact of High-Quality Teaching

Recent studies have demonstrated the enormous impact of high-quality classroom instruction. For instance, in an analysis of the impact of higher-quality instruction Bembry et al. (1998) found that students enrolled in classrooms offering higher-quality instruction achieved standardized reading tests scores after three years that were approximately 40 percentile ranks higher than students enrolled in classrooms with lower-quality instruction. In the Pressley et al. (2000) study of exemplary first-grade teachers, the lowest-achieving students in the exemplary teacher classrooms performed at the same level as the average students in the typical classrooms. These studies, and others like them, simply point to incredible power of providing children with high-quality classroom instruction. In fact, both Ferguson (1991) and Snow et al. (1989) found that nothing was as powerful as the quality of the teacher in predicting the achievement of children. Neither parents nor socioeconomic status of the family were as powerful as good instruction in shaping the academic futures of students.

or resource room program. For too long we have ignored this fundamental aspect of schooling. We have added more support programs, more instructional aides, more specialist teachers, and more computers and software programs, while ignoring the powerful evidence on the importance of high-quality classroom teaching (Allington & Johnston, 2000; Bembry et al., 1998; Ferguson, 1991; Pressley et al., 2000).

So how might improved classroom instruction be accomplished? In my view, it won't be accomplished by purchasing a different basal reader series or by just adding a souped-up technology component (e.g., Waterford Reading, Accelerated Reader, Fast Forward, etc.). It isn't that such tools cannot be useful, but that they simply will not do much to improve teaching quality. Teachers teach what they know and expanding what teachers know produces a substantial impact on students, as Linda Darling-Hammond (1998) noted in summarizing the research on improving teaching.

Supporting Professional Growth

So, a good first step in developing more effective instructional programs for struggling readers is developing a plan for continually upgrading each teacher's expertise (Duffy & Hoffman, 1999). There can be few less organized aspects of education than professional development. School districts have five-year plans for replacing roofs, for upgrading athletic fields, for purchasing buses and new textbooks. But the same districts with these longer-term plans for buildings, grounds, textbooks, and transportation rarely have a five-year professional development plan—even for new teachers. Few school systems seem very concerned about professional development even though opportunities abound for developing the capacity of teachers to deliver high-quality instruction.

For instance, in most schools teachers are in the building but not with children for two or more hours every day—before school begins, after school ends, during scheduled planning periods, and so on. In most districts little of this time is captured for professional development. Instead, most school districts schedule several professional days before the beginning of the school year and a couple during the school year—the ubiquitous Superintendent's Days—and consider this their professional development investment. Only rarely is there a comprehensive plan for how these days will be used or that target specific instructional competencies that will be fostered. Teachers routinely complain about the ineffectiveness of such experiences. And year after year the same pattern is repeated. Yet every day, all year, teachers could be supported in their learning. It is time to rethink professional development.

Most teacher learning occurs on the job, not at workshops. My point here isn't to argue against the traditional workshop as much as it is to argue for a much broader conceptualization of how we might foster the development of teacher expertise (Richardson, 1994). And I would suggest that professional development should be a personal professional responsibility as well as an organizational responsibility. In other words, each teacher has a professional responsibility to continue to become more expert with every year of teaching. Each district has an organizational responsibility to support the professional development of each member of the faculty.

Every school system, or its teachers, should consider these two alternatives to the traditional "talking head" workshop approach to professional development: teachers as professional education readers (TAPER) and teacher inquiry projects (TIP).

Teachers as professional education readers. In TAPER professional development it is professional texts that become a focus for extending professional expertise. Professional books, magazines, or articles are read by the TAPER group and then briefly discussed in a collegial setting.

During the discussion the primary focus is on responding to five questions:

- What was the author arguing for?
- Does the text seem to offer useful ideas for our school/classrooms?
- What do we need more information about?
- Who has tried to implement one or more ideas in their classroom?
- Does it make sense to support additional applications of these ideas?

As with the arguments I made about student book discussions in chapter 5, group members discuss these questions in order to help each other develop deeper and broader understanding of the ideas offered in the books.

I would not suggest that a whole school faculty engage in a single TAPER activity. I can see how a school might have several TAPER initiatives operating at any given point, each with perhaps three to seven members. Someone has to select the text(s) to be read. This could be a group or individual decision (assuming the group is willing to accept the decision of the selector). A period of time for completing the reading is agreed on with a completion date set. Soon after that date the readers agree to meet for a short period (say 30–45 minutes at the end of the school day) and talk together about the text read.

But how will a TAPER group (or group leader) find the texts to read? In many cases, there will be more suggestions than can be easily handled. In other cases one person will have lots of suggestions. And in some cases no one will have a suggested text. The latter is especially true if the TAPER group decides to read on a specific topic (e.g., research on flunking, developing expository writing).

Below are several sources that might be investigated when looking for good professional books:

1. Call or visit your local professional education bookseller and ask for advice.
2. Check out the professional book review columns in educational journals.
3. Brainstorm with each other.
4. Visit websites with professional book reviews (teachersread.com; reading.org; ncte.org; and ldonline.org all offer reviews of books on literacy education).

When recommendations have been gathered, you might want to visit websites of booksellers for additional reviews (amazon.com and bn.com, for instance, offer teacher reviews, primarily, of educational texts). In an ideal world, school district budgets would include funds for purchasing TAPER books (Allington & Cunningham, 2001). However, not all of us work in ideal school districts (or universities). Still, I have found school and district administrators generally receptive to the idea of allocating funds for professional texts when they are approached with a TAPER project plan that indicates the books to be read and the group members. Begin small, with perhaps one book in the fall, another in spring semester, and a third to read over the summer.

Just don't select traditional textbooks for TAPER activities. Many texts meant for the college textbook market suffer from the same limitations that traditional content area textbooks have suffered from—they are too broad, too shallow, and written with no voice. Luckily the past decade has seen explosive growth in powerful professional texts. Texts that are readable, engaging, and practical. Often these texts focus on a slice of literacy and classroom life rather than attempting to "cover the field." Often they are a bit sassier than the droll textbooks we all read as undergrads.

The goal of TAPER activities is to develop individual expertness and foster the development of shared knowledge among members of the group. Some have complained that TAPER activities are too unstructured for their tastes. I will suggest that too often too much structure—all-day workshops with one presenter for a K–12 faculty, for instance—has been the real problem. Teachers within a school differ widely in their expertise, professional needs, commitment to professional growth, and so on. It is as hard to construct a single workshop that meets the needs of all teachers as it is to construct a lesson that meets the needs of all students (imagine designing a single lesson in any subject for a K–12 group of students). Rather than considering TAPER activities unstructured, I'd prefer to think of them as targeted activities that will better meet the needs of a diverse group of professionals.

Teacher inquiry projects. TAPER activities can lead to an interest in TIP activities (though that should not necessarily be designed into a plan). Jeff Wilhelm (1997) describes in detail how his teacher inquiry project provided the understandings he needed in order to restructure his middle-school literacy instruction to better serve the struggling readers he taught. His engaging book-length description of how he changed his instructional practice might serve as the impetus for others to experiment with a similar researching in their classrooms. In many respects, Christie Duthie's (1996) book-length discussion of how she came to see how powerful nonfiction texts can be in developing the reading and writing of primary grade students might serve that same role. In addition, every issue of *Teacher Research* (available from Johnson Press, 49 Sheridan Ave., Albany, NY 12210) contains compelling reports of classroom inquiry projects conducted by teachers. These reports share few features with the sort of research reports one finds in traditional experimental research journals—that is, the reports are personal, readable, moving. In other words, the reading of a book (or a report) in a TAPER activity might prompt readers to develop their own research on the topic, there is no reason to expect that this would typically be the outcome.

I suggest the use of teams in inquiry projects because it is through teamwork that shared knowledge is fostered and professional conversations develop (I find it generally hard to have an extended conversation with myself). Inquiry teams (even two-member teams) provide outside sources for reflection, revision, and interpretation of information. The old "two heads are better than one" idea seems an appropriate way of thinking about researching classroom practice or organizational patterns. And I have become convinced that local research, teacher inquiry, is a necessary component in developing the instructional capacity of teachers. It is the thoughtful reflection on the complications of teaching our students in our classrooms that exposes "quick fix" solutions as largely offering "mythological" advantages. The advantages of TIP activities is in the attempts to "see" more precisely just what the problem is and to evaluate more specifically how shifts in instruction or organization impact those problems. When teams of teachers explore these questions together, a better understanding of the problems and the limitations and complexity of any proposed "solutions" become clearer. One result of this improved clarity can be improved instruction or improved organization of school programs.

A second argument for supporting TIP activities in the quest for improving instruction is that the most powerful source of evidence for the benefits (or lack thereof) of an instructional shift (or a shift in organizational patterns) is the data gathered by teachers in their classrooms. For instance, McGill-Franzen and her colleagues (2000) describe how a teacher inquiry project that focused on the longer-term effects of retention led to a shift in school flunking practices. The availability of a considerable and consistent set of research studies illustrating

---

Teacher Inquiry Projects Guidelines

There are several "hands-on" texts that provide an introduction to TIPs. A TAPER group might want to read one or more of these before beginning a TIP.

Allen, J., Cary, M., & Delgado, L. (1995) *Exploring Blue Highways*. New York: Teachers College Press.

Anderson, G., Herr, K., & Nihlen, A. (1994) *Studying Your Own School: An Educator's Guide to Qualitative Practitioner Research*. Thousand Oaks, CA: Corwin Press.

Hubbard, & Powers, B. (1999) *Teacher Research*. Newark, DE: IRA. (reading.org).

Mohr, M. & McLean, M. (1987) *Working Together: A Guide for Teacher-Researchers*. Urbana, IL: NCTE. (ncte.org).

---

the negative impact of retaining students (c.f., Shepard and Smith, 1989) was unconvincing to many faculty members in this school. But when the longer-term impact of retention on "their" students was examined, the evidence, also negative, was considered important enough to shift away from the widely practiced tradition of flunking students.

Professional conversation. In our research on effective schools, it has been the number and quality of professional conversations available that predicted teacher development (Johnston et al., 1998). Most of these professional conversations were private and personal. Most were one-to-one or small-group conversations about teaching. In the schools we studied that had better adapted instruction to meet the needs of struggling readers more professional conversations occurred and they involved, overall, many members of the faculty. In the schools that were floundering in their efforts to meet the needs of struggling readers we found fewer conversations involving far fewer teachers.

So what accounted for the differences? Well, the more successful, more conversational schools had more decentralized decision-making. In other words, teachers made more decisions about curriculum, instruction, and assessment—teams, clusters, committees, and task forces of teachers decided much of the what and how of instruction. In the less successful, less conversational districts, teachers were more often told what they would do—in some cases, down to which pages in which textbooks would be completed on which days!

When teachers work under conditions of low autonomy they do not seem to develop the very expertise that will be necessary to teach expertly. Under such conditions many teachers simply follow the rules and offer a standard form of instruction. But no school ever became an effective school by having teachers follow a script or having teachers provide a standard form of instruction.

I believe the evidence on the power of professional conversation in developing teacher expertise is sufficient to warrant initiatives that work to foster more such conversation. While TAPER and TIP activities generate professional conversation there are other ways to get folks talking productively with each other. Thus, the following three ideas should be considered if little professional conversation exists in your school (Allington & Cunningham, 2001).

- *Hold faculty or grade-level team meetings in classrooms.* At the beginning of the meeting have the "teacher-host" give a five-minute tour of his or her room. This simply involves pointing out work areas, student projects, special displays, neat ideas, and such. Then the meeting proceeds as normal. This public sharing opens the door to further conversation about the classroom environment, teaching practices, projects, and the like.
- *Hold grade-level team meetings at least weekly.* These can be before school, after school, or during a combined planning period (assuming the school has common planning blocks across grade levels). The main topic of conversation is who is doing what this week. This strategy again produces greater shared knowledge, which by itself increases professional conversation among teachers of the same grades.
- *Web-based lesson plans.* In some schools, teachers now post their weekly (or longer) lesson plans on the school's website. This is often done so that parents can access the lessons and see what sort of assignments their children have. But these lesson plans can also serve as a basis for professional conversation among teachers, especially if collegial lesson plan review or collegial planning is an expected responsibility.

Schools that improve over time foster collegial sharing and support. Enhancing the frequency and usefulness of the professional conversations in your school is a good first step to becoming a school that serves all children better.

Class Size

There is now good evidence that smaller classes, at least in elementary schools, make better teaching possible. This is the primary reason why children in smaller classes demonstrate higher achievement (Achilles, 1999). But smaller classes with more expert teachers in better organized schools produce higher achievement than smaller classes with less expert teachers in schools that are badly managed. Smaller classes produce larger achievement gains in children from low-income families than with more advantaged children—not a surprising finding.

If schools are to develop high levels of reading and writing proficiency in virtually all children, then funding schools so that class sizes of twenty or so are common would be a good first step. But smaller classes are even more effective when the teacher is more expert about teaching children to read and write.

Access to appropriate instructional materials

Effective instruction is characterized by adaptation of the standard form of instruction in ways that better meet the needs of individual students. For example, too many curricular plans are organized around the "single source" curriculum material. In these plans every student has the same curriculum materials, regardless of their level of proficiency. In reading plans of this sort, every child reads in the same basal reader or the same tradebook. In social studies plans of this sort every child reads from the same social studies textbook. In spelling every child works with the same spelling book. I know of no evidence that suggests that any curriculum plan that had all children working in the same books all day, all week, all year, ever produced high achievement in all children, or even in most children.

A key to effective classroom reading lessons is "finding books that fit" the various children. Chapter 3 provided an extensive discussion of the scientific research available on the importance of this principle. Developing expertise in "fitting" the books to children might be one important focus of professional conversations. Most teachers have received some initial training on how to assess the match between books and children but often teachers have worked in schools where the organizational mandate was the single-source lesson plan—everybody in the same book. When confronted with twenty-five students and twenty-five copies of the same text- or tradebook, it isn't surprising that few teachers seemed to use the book-matching skills they had learned. So, we might begin by focusing on supporting teaching within a multisource, multilevel lesson plan.

I will repeat that while school plans might have some common texts that all students use, my advice is that common texts—single-source lessons—be used no more than 20–30 percent of the time. And when common texts are used, teachers must still adapt instruction so that these texts are accessible to all students. There are a variety of techniques that teachers can use to this end. Shared reading, reading the text to students as they follow along, audiotape recordings of the texts, and so on all can work to enhance the usefulness of more difficult texts to lower-achieving students.

Supplying classrooms with books that fit the students may not necessarily require more money to be spent on texts. When schools adopt the book room plan, easy access to a large supply of different texts becomes economical. When schools order fewer copies of a larger number of texts, variety is increased while expenditures are not. But when education dollars are allocated to purchase 100 copies of single fifth-grade basal or social studies text, there is often little money left to expand the supply of texts available. Likewise, when every fourth-grade teacher receives 25 copies of the same four tradebooks, there is often little money left to expand the variety of books. Thus, a first step in creating effective, adaptive classrooms is planning for using available funding to enhance the variety of texts available. We should not be surprised to find teachers planning single-source lessons or series of lessons if the school has allocated its funds to fill every classroom with multiple copies of the same book.

Honoring Instructional Time

So once we have the variety of texts needed to plan multilevel, multisource lessons and once the teachers have refined their "fitting" techniques, we can get on with effective teaching. But such teaching will also take time—blocks of uninterrupted time. The school schedule may need adjustment so as to capture as much of the academic time as is possible. If we can organize schools intelligently and protect every minute of official instructional time—no attendance taking, no milk, lunch, book, or candy sales money collecting, no public address announcements, no unpacking or packing up to leave during the instructional day—we can expand the time teachers have to teach well.

Summary

All this seems minimally necessary in order to create effective classrooms. Teachers need support in order to become more expert with every year of teaching. In my view it is an organizational responsibility to provide such support every single day of the school year. Similarly, teachers cannot be expected to adapt and differentiate their lessons if they are provided with lots of copies of a single text and almost no other books. Nor can teachers be expected to design school days so that much reading and writing is accomplished if they have few books and an instructional day that is effectively reduced in length by bad organizational plans, plans that nibble away, and sometimes gobble up, instructional time. Schools must be organized so teachers and students have every possible minute needed for instruction. None of this is rocket science. All of it is based in scientific studies of effective schools, classrooms, and teachers.

ENHANCING ACCESS TO INTENSIVE, EXPERT INSTRUCTION

Once we are satisfied that the basic organizational responsibilities for creating effective classroom instruction are in place (multiple curriculum materials, effectively operating school schedule, reasonable class size) planning for enhancing students' access to intensive, expert instruction is the next logical step. It makes little sense, however, to focus on this aspect of schooling without also focusing on effective classroom instruction. The purpose of support programs offering intensive, expert instruction should be to meet the needs of those children who will need more than effective classroom teaching in order to learn to read well. If ineffective classroom instruction is contributing to the problem of low achievement, fix that problem directly. Support programs should not be viewed as a way of bypassing the problem of ineffective classroom teaching. But even with effective classroom instruction some students will need more expert and more intensive instruction than we can expect classroom teachers to provide.

We can expect that classroom instruction will be adapted to better meet the needs of low-achieving students. Such adaptations will be helpful but often they are insufficiently intense or insufficiently expert to accelerate struggling readers' reading development.

Intensity. I think of intensity primarily in terms of teacher-pupil ratio, scheduling, and pacing. On the first feature, tutoring tops the intensity scale. Very small group instruction comes next in intensity. The evidence available indicates that both tutoring and very small-group instructional support is more commonly effective than the traditional larger-group (4–7 students) remediation (Wasik & Slavin, 1993). Daily support lessons are more likely to impact achievement than lessons scheduled less frequently. Tutoring or very small group lessons that are paced to take advantage of every minute of time available are more effective than lessons that doodle along. And lessons offered by expert teachers are the most commonly effective design.

Thus, if I were to develop an intervention plan that provided struggling readers with more intensive instructional support, I'd organize the intervention around these principles. But for such a plan to work, classroom instruction would have to be genuinely effective for most students, including the struggling readers. The intervention wouldn't replace in effective classroom instruction but expand on effective classroom lessons.

One substantial shift that is needed immediately in most schools is redesigning the use of instructional support personnel such that intensive interventions can be offered. In too many schools for too many years (Allington, 1987), the reading teachers, resource teachers, speech therapists, and special program paraprofessionals have been assigned to work nonintensively with kids who need intensive interventions. In other words, I commonly see Title 1 reading teachers working with fifty students a week in groups of seven or more. These groups meet briefly, thirty minutes seems common, every other day or so. The same pattern is often repeated with special education teachers and other specialists. But one reason such plans hardly ever produce the sorts of gains we hope for is that the intensity is so low that little benefit can be expected.

Instead of working all year with twenty-five to fifty students in large groups (5–9 students) for a few short sessions each week, consider restructuring the work assignments so that more intensive interventions of less than a year's length are offered. For instance, offer half the students twice as intensive instruction for a single semester. Or offer half a ten-week more intensive intervention and then ten-weeks off followed by another ten-week more intensive intervention. Even Individual Education Plans (IEPs) required for every pupil with a disability can be written to support interventions that offer greater intensity of this sort (300 minutes weekly for a semester rather than 30 minutes daily all year).

Key to more effective support programs is the likelihood that participation will provide access to intensive instructional support designed to quickly accelerate literacy development. Some students will need instruction at a level of intensity that is difficult, if not impossible, to provide in the classroom. Rethinking how we design remedial and special education support is needed in most schools.

Expertness. Every school needs teachers who are more expert on some topics than most teachers. We cannot expect every classroom teacher to be expert on every relevant educational topic. Thus, schools will always need some teachers who are more expert at sorting out why Brittney is struggling with learning to read even with good classroom teaching. Or why Randolph has such a difficult time with fractions. Or how to help Dom control his anger.

However, consider this: If Dom's anger comes from sitting in a classroom where he is confronted all day every day with work he cannot do, then the specialist should not be working with Dom but with his teacher. Dom's anger is justified. If we don't solve the classroom problem that Dom is facing, then we can expect to see more and more children who need anger therapy. In too many schools, the expert teachers are working with the wrong clients—the kids, instead of the teachers. In my view, if the expertise of a reading specialist, a Reading Recovery teacher, or a resource teacher has little impact on improving the quality of classroom instruction across the school, then the expertise is largely wasted. If instructional expertise does not improve the classroom instruction it is typically uneconomical.

We do not need experts who just "fix" kids and return them to ineffective or inefficient classrooms. Sending a "fixed" student back into "broken" classrooms just means that the student will likely need fixing again. Often the student never gets fixed even though provided the usual low-intensity support instruction. Unfortunately, that common finding in the research on remedial and special education programs is not difficult to explain (Glass, 1983).

First, in too many schools the remedial and special education programs are designed so that it will be unlikely there will be any large impact on struggling readers' achievement. Add to that the unfortunate fact that many children served in these program languish daily in classrooms with no appropriately adapted instruction and it is not difficult to see why remedial and special education often have not worked to accelerate reading development of struggling readers (Allington & McGill-Franzen, 1996; Puma et al., 1997).

In school designs where too many students are scheduled for special instruction for too little time, remedial and resource teachers often simply cannot act on their expertise because the limited contact with large numbers means it is unlikely these support teachers know any of their students well. And knowing your students well is critical to good teaching. Many support teachers work with students from twelve to twenty classrooms making coordination with the classroom instruction difficult and collaborative planning with the classroom teacher almost impossible. My point here is simple: We can design interventions that are expensive and unlikely to work even when the intervention personnel are quite expert. Not only *can* we design interventions that are unlikely to be successful, but many schools *do*.

In addition, we often design interventions where the important role of instructional expertise is largely ignored. The now widespread practice of employing paraprofessionals to work with struggling readers is one example of this. There is much evidence that paraprofessionals' lessons rarely exemplify even modestly effective instructional practices and much evidence that because of this struggling readers rarely make much progress when instructed by aides (Achilles, 1999; Allington, 1991; Boyd-Zaharias, 1998; Rowan & Guthrie, 1989). In fact, the research on the use of paraprofessionals is an example of how expensive a bad idea can be. But the numbers of paraprofessionals employed in remedial and special education programs has continued to rise.

Finally, instructional support programs must work to enhance the likelihood that participating students receive larger amounts of appropriate instruction across the school day. In order to achieve maximum progress students need appropriate texts in their hands all day, not just when they are participating in instructional support programs. Thus, one other role for specialist teachers is assisting classroom teachers in locating texts of an appropriate level of difficulty for use in classroom reading, science, and social studies lessons.

Summary

Some students need more expert and more intensive instruction in order for their learning to keep pace with that of other children. Schools must enhance classroom instruction so that the number of struggling readers is minimized and then put into place an organizational strategy that ensures children who need intensive, expert instruction receive it. Ensuring that such services are available will not necessarily be any more expensive than current, less effective, less intensive efforts. The research demonstrates just how powerful expert tutoring is and effective interventions that solve the problems of struggling readers costs less in the long run than less intensive interventions that produce only modest gains.

For instance, much concern about the role of the development of phonemic segmentation in beginning reading has been offered in both the public and professional media in the past few years. My interpretation of the research suggests that while most children develop adequate phonemic segmentation in the course of routine beginning reading instruction, a small proportion of students fail to acquire the understandings and strategies that underlie this skill. These students do not seem to acquire phonemic segmentation from classroom lessons and this lack of development seems powerfully related to their difficulties in learning to read. But the research also points to the power of tutorial and very small group instruction offered by an expert teacher in fostering development of this important skill. In other words, most of the children who fail to develop this skill will develop it with only a few weeks (6–12) of appropriately intensive, expert intervention (Torgeson & Hecht, 1996). A few children may need longer-term interventions but most will not.

What this suggests to me is that schools need to ensure (1) that classroom lessons feature activities that foster development of phonemic segmentation (such as daily invented writing with application of "sound stretching" strategies), (2) an early warning system that identifies those students having difficulty (perhaps monitoring their invented spelling development for evidence of phonemic segmentation), and (3) an intervention plan that ensures that by the middle of the first-grade year any student who has failed to develop this skill is provided with expert, intensive instruction (Allington, 2000; McGill-Franzen et al., 1999; Snow, Burns, & Griffin, 1998; Troia, 1999).

A similar scenario for students who fail to develop self-monitoring, fluency, big-word decoding, narrative comprehension, persuasive composition strategies, and so on should be in place in every school. This sort of targeted assistance, offered more intensively, by expert teachers, should replace the currently popular plan of providing low-intensity, low-expertness, general remediation.

EXPANDING AVAILABLE INSTRUCTIONAL TIME

A second class of intervention plans focus on expanding available instructional time. I have seen three variations within this category. First, there are plans that add a second daily reading lesson during the regular school day. This might be offered by the classroom teacher or by a specialist teacher. It might occur in the classroom or at some other location. Second, are extended day programs where the extra lessons are offered in before- or after-school programs. Again, these lessons might be offered by the classroom teacher or a specialist teacher; although the use of community volunteers has become increasingly popular. Third, are the extended week/extended school year plans. In these plans extra lessons are offered in Saturday School or Summer School settings. Again, the lessons could be offered by classroom or specialist teachers.

The theory behind each of these is one that is linked to the "time-on-task" research reviewed in chapter 2. Fundamentally, the argument is that some children simply need larger quantities of instruction and greater opportunities to practice reading. There is good research evidence that such added instruction can foster accelerated reading development but, again, the most powerful extended time interventions provide more intensive, expert instruction during the added time.

Each of these three classes of extended time efforts should be part of the school plan to meet the instructional needs of struggling readers. In each case, planning such interventions around research-based principles will enhance the likelihood of success.

Adding a Second Daily Lesson

The additional daily instruction might be offered in the classroom by the classroom teacher. In some cases (Cunningham & Allington, 1999; Taylor et al., 1992) this might be offered while other students are engaged in self-selected reading. This seems an especially good time for students who seem unable or unwilling to read independently. But caution is needed because, as you recall, volume of reading is important and if a second reading lesson limits the quantity of reading then the effort seems misguided. However, a second guided reading session has been shown useful, especially in the early grades when independent reading is more difficult because of limited reading proficiencies.

Traditional remedial reading programs were intended to provide a second daily lesson but often did not (Allington, 1987). The federal guidelines for the Title 1 remedial reading program historically required that the remedial lessons "supplement" the daily classroom reading lessons. In other words, the remediation was to be *in addition to* classroom instruction. And classroom instruction was to be adapted to meet the needs of the students who participated in the remedial reading program. However, the research indicated that in many schools this guideline was (and still is) routinely violated. The most common schedule for remedial instruction was during the classroom reading instructional period. Likewise, the most commonly scheduled period for resource room support for pupils identified as learning disabled was during the classroom reading instruction. Thus, in many cases, participating in remedial or special education programs neither increased the quantity of reading instruction nor the volume of reading (Allington, 1984; Allington & McGill-Franzen, 1989; 1996). In addition, the research also indicated that many classroom teachers failed to offer any adaptations to the whole class lessons that were offered. If support instruction fails to expand the amount of reading

Effective Classroom Programs for Struggling Readers

Duffy-Hester (1999) reviewed six research-based classroom reading programs that have been shown to enhance the reading performance of struggling readers. She offered the following ten principles that these programs reflected.

- A reading program should be balanced, drawing on multiple theoretical perspectives.
- There should be a practical and theoretical justification for every component and element in the reading program.
- The explicit teaching of word identification, comprehension, and vocabulary strategies may take place in conjunction with authentic reading and writing tasks.
- On a daily basis, teachers should read aloud to students from a variety of genres and create opportunities for students to read instructional and independent level texts.
- Reading instruction should be informed by and based on meaningful reading assessments.
- Teachers should be decision-makers, using their practical, personal, and theoretical knowledge to inform their reading instruction.
- Staff development for preservice and practicing teachers of reading may include providing opportunities for teachers to reflect on their practice.
- Reading programs may be based on multiple goals for student success; that is, goals as diverse as enhancing voluntary reading, discussion, genre knowledge, and other goals beyond improved test scores.
- Reading programs may provide multiple contexts for student learning; that is, work on multiple types of tasks and engage in multiple talk structures.
- Reading programs should be designed to support the reading growth of all children, both struggling and nonstruggling readers.

instruction, it isn't surprising that many remedial and special education programs produce only small improvements in reading, at best.

Nonetheless, it is possible to design interventions whereby a classroom teacher or specialist teacher provides a second daily reading lesson for struggling readers during the school day. To do this, however, requires making a decision about just what classroom instruction will be replaced by the remedial or special education intervention. In other words, what classroom instructional activities will be sacrificed to provide the second reading lesson? For the second daily lesson to be most effective, it cannot replace part of the classroom reading instruction.

The "after lunch bunch" second reading lesson occurs while most children are engaged in an independent reading activity (Cunningham &

Allington, 1999). Here a second guided reading lesson is offered. But we have to be sure that this lesson is more powerful than "just reading" during independent reading time. Ideally, the after lunch bunch varies on a daily basis with not every struggling reader attending and some not struggling readers involved. In the Early Intervention in Reading (EIR) a second daily twenty-minute reading lesson has also been proven successful in raising the achievement of primary grade students (Taylor et al., 1992). In other projects the reading teacher provides the second lesson in the classroom while the classroom teacher works with other students.

Designing Extended-School-Day Efforts

As states have raised both the achievement standards and the stakes for students (and their teachers) who don't meet those standards, there has been an increased interest in and use of after-school program designs in an attempt to enhance the achievement of struggling readers. There are four basic designs that seem most popular:

- School-based remedial assistance with expert instruction. In this design targeted students work with reading and special education teachers for an hour or more after school to accelerate literacy development.
- School-based tutoring from trained community volunteers, high-school, or college students. These efforts sometimes involve only once or twice weekly sessions although some do provide daily instructional support.
- School-based homework help/child care/recreation with paraprofessional or volunteer support. Here the targeted students work mostly on homework help with the addition of organized and free-play activity with only modest attempts of instruction.
- Community-based homework help/child care/recreation. There are actually fewer school-based than community-based after-school programs currently operating. These programs are sponsored by the YMCA, Boys and Girls Clubs, churches, and other community groups.

I think it is important to acknowledge that we can design after-school programs that produce accelerated reading development. But to achieve this outcome the program has to be well-designed for that purpose. In other words, the key elements of powerful literacy instruction described in the first five chapters are essential in the design of after-school programs. But to develop a powerful after-school program there are a number of issues that need to be addressed.

Staffing.   Not surprisingly, after-school programs where instruction is offered by certified teachers seem more effective in fostering achievement than programs using other staffing patterns. But most after-school programs operate with only one or two certified instructional staff members (Seppanen et al., 1993). One problem, of course, is funding. Use of noncertified staff reduces costs. When after-school programs are focused on homework help, child care, and recreation opportunities, then wider use of noncertified staff may be reasonable. But when accelerating the literacy achievement of struggling readers is the goal, we must be concerned about effectiveness more than inexpensiveness.

There are funding sources for after-school programs that have gone largely untapped. Title 1 funds, for instance, were used to support less than 10 percent of after-school programs (Seppanen, 1993). Special education funds were not even noted as a source. In fact, most after-school programs were funded by parent fees. This may account for the fact that such programs were more common in higher-wealth communities than in the lowest-wealth communities (Halpern, 1999).

Flextime, another strategy for providing certified professional staff for after-school programs seems little used (Allington & Cunningham, 2001). In flextime models a school's specialist teachers—reading, special education, speech therapists, physical education, art, music, and computer teachers—along with other non-classroom teaching staff—librarians, counselors, psychologists—work on a different daily schedule from that the classroom teachers follow. For instance, if the school day begins at 8:00 A.M. and ends at 2:30 P.M., then classroom teachers might arrive at 7:30 and depart at 3:30. Specialist staff, however, might arrive at 9:30 and depart at 5:30. These staff would provide the core staff for an after-school program that would run from 2:30 to 5:30 (though not all students would necessarily remain for the full 3 hours).

While certain staff might be providing tutorial and small-group instructional support during the after-school hours, others would offer recreational activity, homework support, and general supervision. Some of the recreational activity might be linked to the reading instruction provided. For instance, art, drama, or music activities linked to books being read. Physical activity should be a regular component of after-school programs that extend more than an hour in length. The after-school program would have a variety of large-group, small-group, very-small-group, and tutorial activities occurring simultaneously.

Use of community volunteers, paraprofessionals, high school and college student tutors are a common feature in many after-school programs. While Wasik and Slavin (1993) found that programs using certified teachers were substantially more effective than programs using noncertified personnel, others report fairly powerful results with programs staffed by non-certified personnel (e.g. Davidson & Koppenhaver, 1993; Invernizzi, Rosemary, Juel, & Richards, 1997; Wasik, 1998). The key here seems to be providing noncertified personnel with strong training, structured tutorials, and ongoing supervision and support.

For instance, in the *Reading Buddies* after-school program (Invernizzi et al., 1997) community volunteers receive initial training in a four-step tutorial lesson plan. A site coordinator also provides daily lesson planning assistance for each tutor. Site coordinators are certified reading teachers and supervise no more than fifteen volunteer tutors. The tutors follow a forty-five-minute structured lesson format that includes:

- ten to fifteen minutes of rereading a familiar book;
- ten to twelve minutes of word study from a developmental spelling perspective;
- five to ten minutes of writing for sounds; and

Cautionary Advice on Extended-Day and Extended-Year Efforts

Before penalizing children by taking away normal childhood free time, it is incumbent on schools to ensure that very nearly 100 percent of the school day's instruction is appropriate to each child's needs. I would argue that creating after-school or summer school programs is professionally unethical unless we are absolutely sure that all children receive optimal instruction all year long *during* the regular school day. All of us need to focus our primary efforts on ensuring that children have access to high-quality teaching in their classrooms before we consider adding extended-time interventions.

- ten to fifteen minutes on introducing a new book including an echo reading, if needed.

The coordinators select the texts for tutors and identify elements of words that are to be worked on. During tutoring sessions they observe the tutors and later offer advice on improving their instructional activities. The *Book Buddies* program has proven quite successful as part of the Charlottesville, VA schools' commitment to helping every child read on level by third grade. The gains children have made are impressive, especially those who participate in forty or more tutorial sessions. The annual cost is estimated at approximately $600 per student served (this includes a professional wage for the supervisors and materials used).

Davidson and Koppenhaver (1993) describe another successful program that uses high school and college students as tutors in a program targeted at improving the achievement (and ultimately reducing the dropout rate) among Native American elementary school students in a northwestern school district. The two certified instructional staff members train tutors and supervise the tutoring of the seventy-five or so students, mostly fourth through sixth graders struggling with reading. Each student receives two one-hour tutorials each week. Tutors are drawn from local high schools and colleges. They are provided with eight hours of training before they begin tutoring. Again the tutoring sessions are structured for the volunteer tutors (some of whom are former tutees). Tutors work on a particular reading/spelling/writing skill with students (based on analysis of student development by supervisors) for ten to fifteen minutes, then they work on building sight vocabulary of words the student has had difficulty with for another ten minutes; the remainder of the session is spent reading a student-selected book, often in a partner reading format, and discussing the story being read. Each student also receives approximately six books each year through the Reading Is Fundamental program. These books are often the focus of the shared reading. Computers are available for skill-work activities. A variety of educational software can be used or the computer can simply be used as a word processor.

Many of the most effective programs described in the literature have worked hard to create after-school programs that are not only powerful but that look little like the typical school-day lessons. Students seem more often to have the opportunity to choose the material they read. They have up-close and personal interactions with their tutors, and they are more often actively engaged (as opposed to sitting alone passively completing worksheets). One advantage of using community volunteers and high school and college students (besides the inexpensiveness) is that these folks seem to find it easy to deliver instruction that is less formal while still powerful.

Staffing after-school programs is important. Cost is important. But so is the effectiveness of the program in solving the problems of struggling readers. It seems unlikely that we will soon have the funding to provide tutoring from certified, expert teachers to every child who needs it—thus, the importance of thinking hard about how to create after-school programs without a full staff of certified, expert personnel.

Scheduling.   At first glance this seems like a no-brainer. After-school programs are scheduled after the school day ends. But there are other scheduling issues to consider. Will every student be expected to attend every day, or only some days (say, Tuesday through Thursday or Monday through Wednesday)? Will different students be provided different schedules for attendance (some twice weekly, some every day)? Flexibility in scheduling should be a given since some students would seem likely to benefit from more intensive and more frequent attendance and others might do quite well while attending less often. Will every student be tutored every day, or only some of the neediest students with others being tutored twice a week? Will some get tutoring from expert staff and others from volunteers? How will this be decided?

How long will the after-school program run? One hour, two hours, three hours? Will all students stay the full period? What sorts of activities will be available during the after-school program? Will it begin with a large-group aerobics session to allow kids to get active for a few minutes before settling in for lessons or homework help? Will there be a small snack available? Will each day include large-group, small-group, very-small-group, and tutorial sessions? For all or only some kids? Will there be active time as well as quiet time? Social time as well as academic?

I can envision an after-school program that rotates students among large-group, small-group, and tutorial activities throughout a 90- or 120-minute period. I can envision students selecting from art, drama, music, and physical education activities as well as selecting particular themes (e.g., pirates, mammals, mysteries, weather, comic books, scripting, etc.) that they will read and write and create in. I can see large groups of children snuggled about with books or magazines they have selected to read for the next thirty to forty-five minutes. I can see groups of five to seven students working on a script developed from a novel they've read, readying themselves for a short dramatic enactment. All the while some children come and go from their tutoring sessions.

In short, I can envision an after-school program that accelerates literacy development by engaging students in substantial quantities of joyful reading and writing acivities. But few after-school programs currently resemble my envisioned program. I think we can do better than we typically have.

Homework.   Like many others, I worry about creating "pressure cooker" environments that rob children of childhood play time. But I also worry about children who are struggling in their attempts to learn to read—especially given the stakes that are now being tied to failing to attain grade-level achievement (e.g., flunking). Designing after-school programs that balance these concerns is important. I happen to believe that learning to read can be a joyful experience and that after-school programs need to work toward achieving this end. Thus, we have the problem of homework assigned to struggling readers. Homework becomes problematic when it is (1) inappropriately difficult, (2) stultifyingly boring and trivial, and (3) assigned in immense quantities (more than a half hour daily). Such homework becomes a problem because it often interferes with our attempts at providing high-quality instruction in after-school programs.

So what to do about homework? First, check on the appropriateness of the assigned homework for struggling readers attending the after-school program. In an ideal world the homework will be useful and extend the learning opportunities for the student. In such cases, make time in the program for homework completion. This might be either before or after tutoring or small-group instruction designed to accelerate literacy development. Homework completion can be accomplished in a larger-group setting and appropriate homework should not require much assistance.

But when the assigned homework is not appropriate—too much, too hard, too trivial—then I think negotiations with the classroom teacher must be scheduled. The negotiations will differ depending on the problematic aspect of the assigned homework. Replacing the assigned homework with something more appropriate is one possibility. Eliminating the assigned homework in lieu of after-school-linked assignments is another. But spending valuable after-school-program time on inappropriate homework assignments must be avoided.

Summary.   We have a choice. We can create powerful programs that accelerate literacy development or create something else. After-school programs need to be guided by the same principles as effective classroom programs. I would argue that access to appropriate texts, access to powerful, personalized strategy instruction, and the opportunity to select the sorts of texts to be read are critical features of the design of after-school efforts to accelerate literacy development. Perhaps the best measure of the success of after-school programs is the number of children who yearn for the end of the school day so they can go to the after-school program. The nice thing about after-school programs is that they are not constrained by the same sorts of rules and regulations as the typical school-day program is.

So be creative, loosen up. Remember though that acceleration of literacy development is the goal but within a design that fosters engagement and joy.

Crafting Powerful Summer-School Programs

When thinking about summer programs it may be useful to differentiate among possible programs designed to achieve different outcomes. For instance, if we wanted to simply attempt to stem summer reading loss—that phenomenon that seems to primarily impact both lower-achieving readers and students from lower-income communities (Cooper et al., 1996; Puma et al., 1997)—then we might design an intervention that simply increased student access to reading materials over the summer months. On the other hand, if we hoped to accelerate the development of reading and writing proficiency during the summer, then we would design an intervention that provided students access not just to reading materials but also to intensive, expert instruction. And if we simply wanted to keep students entertained (or even just busy) then we might design a program with little attention to enhancing access to either reading materials or expert instruction. In addition, the design would be influenced by many of the same decisions one makes in designing after-school programs—budget, staff, schedule, and so on. In the next sections I want to focus on the design of programs of the first two types—minimizing summer reading loss and accelerating literacy development.

Minimizing Summer Reading Loss

Given the accumulated research evidence on the relationship between access to reading materials and volume of reading and the evidence on the relationship of volume of reading to reading proficiency, it seems obvious that one proactive preventive measure that schools should take is to ensure access to books during the summer months. Remember the data on family socioeconomic status and access to age-appropriate books in the home and at school. Students from lower-income families are those least likely to have easy access to appropriate books in their homes (or their neighborhoods). These students had the most limited access to books in their schools as well (Guice et al., 1996; Smith, Constantino & Krashen, 1997).

Access to school library collections. Thus, I would suggest that the least expensive intervention that a school might offer, especially a school that serves students from lower-income families, is to simply make a supply of school library books available to students over the summer. For instance, any student who so desired might be allowed to check out, say, ten books from the school library for the duration of the summer. But parents with few financial resources will be wary of allowing their children such a privilege if they worry about a potentially large bill should the books be damaged or lost. Schools could set up "night return" receptacles such as those found at most public libraries and video stores. Then students could return books as they were completed, which should stem some losses. But I believe we worry too much about protecting books from children. Allow the children to take the books and hope for the best.

A better suggestion, of course, would be to keep the library open during the summer, at least one or two days each week. In this case students could check out one or two books each visit, which would again minimize loss as well as provide access to more books over time. But keeping the library open during the summer adds costs not present when students simply check out summer reading books on the last day of school. Still, a handful of schools across the country keep their libraries operating during the summer months—perhaps 1 of every 100 or so school libraries based on the responses of teacher-audiences I've asked over the past few years. But if we adopted flextime models we might close the library on Mondays during the school year but use those staff days to open the library four days a week over the summer. Thus, the school librarian would work no more days but would work the contractual days across the whole year, not just during the traditional academic year.

Another strategy would be to distribute classroom paperback collections to students for summer reading. But you may need to open up selection so students can choose books from all classroom libraries. This won't be a popular idea if many of the books in classroom libraries are teacher-purchased and if classroom libraries vary substantially because of that. Nonetheless, the importance of access to books is great enough to ask why any school-purchased books should remain in the building over the summer if there are students who want to read them and who have little other access to books.

If we were a bit more ambitious (and had a bit more money) we might consider promoting "reading clubs" during the summer months and organize opportunities for students to meet and talk about the books they've read. We might link this to opportunities to perform—reenact scenes, display artwork developed from the reading, or skits and plays motivated by the books read. We could have students post reviews on the World Wide Web at any of the several sites that encourage such responses from young readers. Developing these ideas would be done largely at home not at school, though in some cases the school might need to provide some of the materials or equipment or a space to rehearse. Staffing could be kept to a minimum in such a design, especially if older student volunteers are available to assist younger children in their discussions and projects.

Access to Books of Their Own.   We might consider just gifting books to children to read over the summer, ideally allowing children to choose the books they will get. Of course such a plan would require funding to purchase the books. However, with resources such as the inexpensive books distribution program a school could provide each student with two paperbacks for a dollar or two per student. Or we could elect to implement a summer reading program modeled after the Sweet Home (NY) school district plan, a gift certificate redeemable at a local branch of a national bookstore chain, though we might have to offer transportation to the bookstore for some children (and their parents). Each student could be asked to donate one of the books purchased back to the school after it had been read to build book collections for future use. We could encourage students to trade books with other students after they had read them to increase the number of books available to each student.

Personally, I can't imagine any better expenditure of curriculum materials funds. The huge array of books in these book superstores, when combined with their student discounts, produces a powerful setting for helping almost any child find a book that begs to be read. Imagine if on the opening day of summer school (or the day before summer vacation begins) all students were bussed to such a bookstore, given such gift certificates and two hours to shop. Imagine the excitement for the student who has no books of his or her own at home, who attends a school where classroom libraries are virtually nonexistent, and where the school library is closed all summer.

There are other variations on this theme:

- My local Gainesville (FL) paper just reported on a similar project that provided every child, all 540 of them, with a summer book on the final day of school. In this case one teacher worked to recruit donations, many from the small business community.
- A Michigan school I visited offered a book fair during the last week of school and the PTA funded one free book for every student whose parents did not send in the requested $3.00.
- At another Florida high-poverty school the principal developed a "free library" at the school's entrance. Here there was a display of a supply of paperbacks that students could just take with them as they left the building, including books for the summer from an enhanced supply provided in the final week of school. The books for the free library came from a variety of sources including the inexpensive books programs, student-donated books, teacher- and community-donated books, and some purchased books.
- A Wisconsin school requested parents donate any children's books that were no longer being used and then filled a table with the donations so that on the final day of school students could pick up two books to read over the summer. The project is so successful that the free book table is now a permanent fixture at the school entrance.

I think the evidence is clear that:

- some students have few books or other reading materials at home;
- easy access to reading materials enhances the likelihood that students read;
- students who read more frequently become more proficient readers and writers; and
- summer reading loss is attributable, in part, to limited reading activity.

Thus, it would seem to me that efforts to increase students' access to books during the summer months would be a priority in schools where many students have limited access to books and other reading materials outside of school. Ideally, the books made available would be books that had a high level of attractiveness to target students. That is, series books, cartoon books, scary books, popular culture books (e.g., *Pokemon*, *Star Wars*, *Dawson's Creek*), informational books, and the like may be more attractive than award-winning literature. This isn't an argument to deny access to great literature as much as it is a plea to consider student interests when planning for voluntary summer reading support.

Accelerating Literacy Development

Developing plans to stem summer reading loss seems like a good idea to me. But some students need more than this. In fact, increasingly, students are being mandated to attend summer school because their reading proficiency falls below some normative cutoff point. These students often see summer school as a personal penalty for something over which they had little control. Unfortunately, in too many cases they seem to be right. When students who find learning to read more difficult attend schools where little intensive, expert assistance is provided during the school year, it isn't surprising that many end up falling behind. When falling behind means you have to forego your summer vacation it isn't surprising that some students resent the imposition. Imagine if these new regulations included the requirement that the teachers who taught students who failed to read well enough were also mandated to attend summer school—to teach in the summer with no additional salary stipend. It wouldn't surprise me if more than a few of the teachers were disgruntled and thought this plan was unfair.

My point here is that mandatory summer school attendance isn't the most motivating basis for showing up at the classroom door. But here is the tricky part: Summer school programs for such students need to be both engaging *and* powerfully instructional. In fact, it is difficult to achieve the latter without the former. I worry that sometimes we attend more to the engaging aspect than the powerful instruction aspect (not all engaging things are powerfully instructional, watching the Cartoon Channel or Jerry Springer or playing basketball, actual or video, for example). Or we get caught up in the myths of skill-drill and worksheet activities. We then create summer schools that reflect the worst of traditional remedial and special education programs.

What worries me is the design of summer school programs that are neither engaging nor instructionally powerful. For instance, creating a program where paraprofessionals supervise struggling readers completing piles of phonics worksheets and then engaging in round-robin oral reading of inappropriately

---

According to Public Agenda's "Reality Check '99" Survey

Most students (61 percent) agree with the statement that "summer school is serious." But 35 percent say kids in summer classes "are not expected to learn much."

http://www.publicagenda.org/specials/rcheck/rcheck.htm

difficult texts followed by regular spelling tests on words the students can't read, much less spell, and closing with another pile of grammar/punctuation/contractions worksheets. Sad to say, but this is not ficticious poorly designed summer school but, rather, one I had been asked to informally evaluate because attendance was poor, discipline problems were rampant, and not surprisingly, little academic progress was observed as a result of participation.

I would like to think that the educator who designed this summer school was simply ignorant as opposed to mean-spirited. In my short evaluation of the program I asked why anyone would have thought such a design would have had a positive effect on achievement. Think about the research-based principles presented in this book. Not one was represented in that summer program. So what might a research-based summer school program designed to accelerate reading development look like?

Expert Instruction.   Students who struggle to acquire reading proficiency need more expert instruction than other students. Expert instruction is more likely from a well-trained teacher than from a volunteer or paraprofessional. That doesn't mean that volunteers and paraprofessionals have no role in summer programs but that we cannot expect them to provide the expert instruction that struggling readers will need to accelerate their literacy development. That is, volunteers and aides might supervise larger groups of students during independent reading blocks or organize and support a Reader's Theater activity or work to help students select new books. They might even listen to younger readers read aloud, after training in the PPPP strategy for how to listen and support that reading.

Students don't necessarily need up-close and personal expert instruction over the whole summer school day, though. Here again, we should think flexibly in the design of a summer school day. I think that a mix of large-group, smaller-group, very-small-group or tutorial activities should be part and parcel of summer school days. For instance, in a three-hour morning summer school day (8:00 A.M. to noon with 30 minutes for breakfast and a 30-minute recess), I would insist on the following:

- Large-group sessions where students read or write independently for blocks of time (45–90 minutes) once or twice each day. These could be supervised by paraprofessionals.
- Smaller-group sessions for guided reading and writing lessons, for collaborative student projects, book discussions, and so on that might last for 60 minutes. The instructional session would be conducted by teachers and the project work, perhaps, by paraprofessionals. The hour could be split between a guided reading lesson and a related project activity, for instance.
- Very-small-group sessions (2–3 students) or tutorials that every struggling reader would participate in daily for 30 minutes. Two types of such activities—expert instructional and personalized practice—should be available with expert teachers offering the former and well-trained and supervised paraprofessionals or volunteers managing the latter.

Struggling readers need powerful summer instruction if we hope to accelerate literacy development in any substantial way. Most summer school programs last eight to ten weeks, and we don't expect much growth during the school year in that period of time. Getting serious about accelerating reading and writing development in a summer school program means that we need a daily design that produces, perhaps, twice the reading and writing these students would do during a normal school day. The research-based principles offered in this book should guide the design of summer programs—but remember the brevity factor: Only with intensive and engaging instruction can we expect to accelerate reading and writing proficiency in a few weeks.

Engaging instruction. The problem that we confront in designing summer school programs looks something like this:

1. Students who have experienced difficulty in learning to read and write often demonstrate less enthusiasm for reading and writing than their peers who learned to read and write more easily and successfully.
2. These struggling readers and writers often demonstrate this diminished enthusiasm by avoiding reading and writing activity whenever possible and, so are less likely to elect to voluntarily read and write or to demonstrate sustained engagement even during mildly coercive reading and writing activities such as Drop Everything and Read.
3. And this is the targeted group of students who will be most likely to (a) benefit from voluntary reading to stem summer reading loss, and (b) be mandated to attend summer school to improve their reading and writing proficiency.
4. But in order to stem summer reading loss or accelerate literacy development, our summer program design (or after-school program, for that matter) must involve these students in a substantial volume of reading and writing activity (Carpenter & Pearson, 1999).

So, in addition to the access and the expert instruction our program effectiveness will turn on how successful we are in enticing our students to read and write a lot. My point here is that I think we have too long underestimated the importance of creating intervention programs focused primarily on fostering increased student engagement with books, magazines, and other texts.

Designing programs that foster voluntary engagement in reading actually does not seem so difficult. But the design is quite different from the traditional remedial or special education intervention design. A first difference is that a primary initial focus is finding out just what interests the student rather than finding out which "skills" the student lacks. Thus, an entry assessment might include an interview rather than a diagnostic test. The interview would focus on interests, hobbies, talents, and favorite school subjects and genres of texts. We might even interview the student's classroom teacher or parents for insights into his or her interests and talents.

The results of this interview would be treated just as diagnostic test information is typically treated, as information useful in planning a summer program. We will also need to develop a good sense of the student's current

---

Preliminary Interview: Gathering Information on Interests

Tell me about any hobbies you have or sports you play.
What are your favorite TV programs? Video games?
Can you think of one book you really liked?
Are there any particular authors whose books you like?
Are there magazines, cartoons, or comic books that you like?

---

reading level, although, again, his or her classroom teacher, the school testing program, and the interview with the student should all provide information of this sort.

In addition to an interview, I would recommend that the opening day or two of summer school provide multiple opportunities for students to select reading material from a wide range of texts. Thus, I would organize collections of books of varying levels of difficulty by genre (e.g., mystery, historical fiction, biography), popular content themes (e.g., dinosaurs, pyramids, Native American peoples, machines), and popular culture topics (e.g., wrestling, sports, television shows, entertainers, favorite series such as *Arthur* or *Sweet Valley High*, trends such as *Pokemon*). Provide multiple and extended opportunities for students to select materials from these books and magazines. Have a paraprofessional or volunteer keep track of choices each student makes. Mingle with the students as they select materials and sit to read them (or try to).

Several times every day "bless" a few books by holding them up and telling just a bit about them or by reading a page or two from them. If the students find books that they get excited about have them discuss and praise those books in front of other kids. Remember that most adults and most good readers get most of their recommendations for reading materials from friends and peers.

After the first day or two each summer the schoolteacher should be plagued by questions like: Where can I find another book or two on snakes written at a second-grade level? Books on the Battle of Gettysburg at the fourth-grade level? The resources offered earlier in this book will provide sources for finding needed books but don't forget to turn to other teachers (in the cases above, the school's second- and fourth-grade teachers might be sources).

If truth be told, though, you are likely going to have to convince some students of their interest in a particular book or genre, or topic. In other words, part of the job will be kindling a spark of interest in reading certain texts. This becomes part of the job for two reasons. First, some students have high avoidance levels due to repeated failures with reading. Second, you will want to cluster students for guided reading and writing activities, and for very small group lessons. While not every guided reading/writing lesson or small group support lesson requires that all students have read a common text, use of a common text is the typical format for such instructional settings.

Most good teachers are also good actors and so exhibiting enthusiasm for certain books is not that difficult to pull off (besides, you can always select common texts from the books you really do like). In addition, reading a bit of the book (or more than a bit) will often create an interest where none existed. Offering what we dubbed "managed choice" is another strategy that the exemplary teachers we observed routinely initiated (Allington & Johnston, 2000). Managed choice meant that students typically had several texts to choose from and, at times, had to come to a group agreement on which book they would read for the group sessions. At other times, students would select different books, sometimes with two kids choosing one and three others selecting a different option. The managed choice often involved choosing a book from a selection of books on a content topic or from a particular genre. As Guthrie et al. so amply demonstrated (1997), this sort of integrated planning produced greater interest and engagement in reading than did the traditional "everyone reads the same reader selection" design.

But books aren't the only texts that should be used. Magazines are another powerful source for engaging reading materials. So too is the Internet. When students are reading on a content theme especially, the Internet provides another ready supply of reading materials. That there already exist a number of websites that provide students with a wealth of information on content themes (and other topics of interest to kids and adolescents) can only be viewed as a positive. Many adults worry that the Internet will undermine the power of reading but I hold just the opposite view. Few websites offer information in a manner that makes reading proficiency irrelevant.

Many websites offer a "real world" educational activity that involves reading and writing. The Audubon Society has operated a website, for instance, where students (K–12) living in areas where migratory birds travel count and record the birds they have seen. This creates a data bank that students can use to predict when certain birds will appear in their area. At a school in the Panhandle region of Florida elementary students operate an Internet project called, Keepers of the Coast. The students in Gulf Coast communities track a variety of aspects of the coastal environment and learn about everything from wildlife, to ecology, to industry in the region. They read information, much of it from websites, and write information, some posted on websites, as part of this project.

In addition, computers provide students with the tools to write better and to produce reports and stories that are incredibly more sophisticated and interesting than the paper-pencil research report. The use of software such as HyperStudio, PageMaker, and lots of other desktop publishing and performance software can engage students who never thought writing was very interesting before.

Of course, engaging instruction is also instruction where the students have books they can read accurately, fluently, and with at least general comprehension. But one real challenge we face in the design of summer school programs is that of engaging the student and enticing him or her to voluntarily read and write both in school and out. My concern is that students who are mandated to

Websites that Satisfy Curiosity (and Reading)

There are lots of appropriate reading material on the web, some of it is even linked to school subjects. There is no way to begin to list all the interesting websites but just as examples, visit this diverse collection of sites.

www.discoveryschool.com   Brought to you by the Discovery Channel with lots of geography, history, and science stuff for kids, this site includes games and virtual trips around the world.

www.insects.org   Advertised as "shameless promotion of insect appreciation," this site will kindle the curiosity of any kid, and especially those wondering about "that bug" they've just found.

www.enature.com   This is a National Audubon Society site that allows you to search for reports and images of almost 5,000 species.

www.co.fairfax.va.us/library/homepage.htm   Here the Fairfax County Library in Virginia offers links to "Good Reading" for preschool-age children through adults.

www.ala.org/yalsa/about/vision.html   Click on "Young Adult Sites" on the menu on the right side of this home page to reach "Teen Hoopla," an Internet site for teens, where they can vote for their favorite book and submit a book review.

www.zamboni.com   Just as it says, this site is dedicated to the Zamboni (that machine that resurfaces the ice at hockey games). One of my sons long aspired to be a Zamboni driver and here he could have read about the Zamboni driver of the year!

---

attend summer school might reasonably be expected to resist engaging very often and, instead, work harder at creatively avoiding engaging in reading and writing. Thus, our design problem is crafting powerful summer interventions that entice struggling readers to engage in the one activity that will accelerate achievement, lots of reading.

AVAILABILITY OF SUPPORT ACROSS THE SCHOOL CAREER

There has been much recent emphasis on early intervention in an attempt to foster greater early school success. Various politicians have set goals such as all children reading on level by third grade. The thinking behind the early intervention push was stimulated by research that indicated that many children who experienced early difficulties in reading never recovered (Juel, 1994). At the same time there have been several studies of substantial gains made by older readers when they have access to expert, intensive instruction (Krashen, 1993; Morris, Ervin & Conrad, 1996; Davidson & Koppenhaver, 1993). My worry is that some educators and policy makers assume that early intervention programs will largely solve the problem of struggling readers. That is, if we could get all students off to a successful start there would be no need for later instructional support programs. But the literature is replete with studies showing that many children make adequate early progress in reading development only to experience difficulties later on.

There is the notorious "fourth-grade hump" (Chall, 1983), so called because at that grade level some children who had been making good progress begin to experience difficulties. Some attribute this to the growing use of informational texts that are often poorly written and present topics of which most children have little prior knowledge. Others suggest that it is the problem of encountering a growing supply of "big words" (Cunningham, 1999): words that present decoding difficulties if children are still trying to "sound out" words letter by letter (e.g., vignette, ideologies, mysogeny, plateau, metamorphosis, inclement). The reader also encounters more easily decodable words that are often wholly new to the reader in that they are words that have never been heard before (pact, irony, delta, thrive, Moors). There seems also to be a "middle school hump" in that too many successful elementary school readers exhibit little growth in reading proficiency during the middle school years (Snow et al., 1991). At the high school level (and beyond) even more students encounter their first real difficulties with reading.

I think it is critical that we recognize that there will always be students who will need continued support instruction beyond that provided in early intervention programs and that we create later intervention programs that provide older struggling readers access to expert, intensive instruction. I also think traditional notions about how to design such programs need to be reconsidered. For instance, Walmsley (1981) suggested that interventions for older struggling readers fall into one of four philosophical categories.

- *Romantic*. These programs would emphasize reading engagement and reading for personal fulfillment and empowerment. This could be a voluntary drop-in-and-discuss-what-you've-read program, or any program that focuses on voluntary, personal reading and responses to that reading. Instruction is likely to be offered but perhaps only when invited. Reading makes us human.
- *Utilitarian*. In these programs the focus is often on career enhancement or preparation of the real world and workplace literacy. Students might practice reading want ads or completing employment applications or studying manuals and technical writing. Reading makes you employable.
- *Cognitive/constructivist*. The focus of these programs is often to help students better deploy reading proficiencies in academic learning settings. There might be instruction on study skills, content text-reading strategies, and writing research papers or the traditional five-part essay. Reading makes you more successful in school.
- *Behaviorist*. Many remedial and special education interventions for struggling readers have long reflected a behaviorist approach with instruction focusing on decoding and spelling accuracy and completion

of lots of low-level skills texts meant to provide practice on the imagined subprocesses of reading and writing. Reading real books is typically not a dominant theme in these designs. Reading self-selected books is even less common. Students may have reward schedules for both work completion and behavioral management. Reading is work and you should be rewarded for doing it.

My hunch is that "pure" examples of such program categories are relatively rare. I would also suggest that most intervention developers never thought much about the larger philosophical underpinnings of their programs. Personally, I am an eclectic in these matters most of the time. Programs should be designed to fit the needs of struggling readers and I can imagine older readers who would benefit differently from programs of different types. I don't have much confidence in behaviorist approaches if only because we have tried such approaches for such a long time with so little success. Of course, some struggling readers may need instruction targeted at developing one or more of the subprocesses of reading. But at this point in my career I am quite convinced by the evidence that traditional behavioral approaches have limited utility in developing readers and writers.

If we expect all students to meet the sorts of academic standards that fewer than half of the students have historically met—and that is precisely what many of the new state high school graduation standards set as the goal—then school programs for older struggling readers will have to include plans for providing some students with access to extraordinarily intensive and expert instructional support throughout their school careers. In addition, two types of support will be needed.

Enhancing Access to Appropriate Texts.   The documented decline in voluntary reading that begins in the middle school years (Foertsch, 1992) seems, in no small part, related to a widening gap in the availability of appropriate materials—both curriculum materials and school-linked access to texts on topics of interest. As Chall and Conard (1991) noted, the increased reliance on single texts for courses increases the likelihood that students encounter texts they cannot read. The recent study of science textbooks adds to the evidence by demonstrating just how difficult many such texts are relative to student reading development. But it may be

---

Resources for Reluctant Teen Readers

Rip-roaring reads for reluctant teen readers, Libraries Unlimited (www.lu.com).
More rip-roaring reads for reluctant teen readers, Libraries Unlimited .
Kids' favorite books and *More kids' favorite books*. IRA (reading.org).
High-interest, easy reading: A booklist for middle school and high school. (ncte.org).

the critical decline in access in school to reading materials considered interesting that contributes more to the fall off in voluntary reading.

Both Ivey (1999) and Worthy and McCool (1996) report huge gaps between what early adolescents report they like to read and what is available in middle and high school libraries and classrooms. They also note that there were few occasions for self-selection of reading materials—teachers almost always assigned reading materials and rarely was there time set aside in school for independent reading. Ivey also notes that attitudes toward reading were often powerfully shaped by the nature of the classroom environments.

In earlier sections I offered a number of examples of just how a school might enhance the likelihood that students would choose to read outside of school. While many of the examples I offered were drawn from elementary schools, I would note that that was due more to the limited number of such efforts found at the middle and high school level than to limited need for such efforts with adolescents. Yes, even middle and high school programs should worry about the extent, or lack of, of voluntary reading. If most students in your middle or high school do not read much on their own, it may be a good time to evaluate just what features of the school program are missing or misguided. If struggling middle and high school students in your school experience a steady diet of hard, boring (in their view) books, there is no reason to be surprised that they exhibit little in the way of literacy development (and academic progress) during the middle and high school years.

Maintaining/Accelerating Literacy Development.   First, the evidence now available indicates that some students will only achieve such standards with long-term literacy support. Such support will almost necessarily have to come from teachers with expertise in meeting the instructional needs of adolescents struggling with literacy learning. My point is that even with high-quality classroom instruction throughout the K–12 span and intensive, expert literacy intervention, some students will continue to find literacy acquisition a more difficult task than most of their peers. Historically we have labeled such students dyslexic or learning disabled and then largely abandoned attempts to teach them to read. But we developed what I have termed "bypass" instruction and what others have termed "accommodations." That is, we provided these students with audiotaped recorded texts, note takers, and aides who read their texts and tests to them and we often lowered the academic goals we expected these students to achieve.

For instance, there is little evidence in the research on middle-school and high school special education programs that suggests that intensive, expert reading instruction is routinely offered to pupils with disabilities (Kos, 1991). At the same time, when such instruction is provided, many of these students exhibit substantial acceleration in the development of their reading skills. Too few adolescents attend schools that offer intensive remedial programs (and even when these programs are available pupils with disabilities often are deemed ineligible). But again we have good evidence that intensive, expert reading interventions can accelerate the reading development of adolescent

---

High School Reading Course Produces Big Gains

Bev Showers and Bruce Joyce with their colleagues (1998) describe the implementation of a daily reading course built into an urban, multi-ethnic high school curriculum that students took in lieu of other electives. Key components of the course included:

- reading appropriate books in school and at home;
- listening to teachers read good literature;
- instruction in active comprehension strategies;
- building vocabulary through reading;
- phonics and structural analysis training; and
- building vocabulary through natural language use.

Each semester students read five to six books matched on difficulty and interest. Both whole-group and small-group lessons on comprehension and structural analysis strategies are offered along with a daily read-aloud by the teacher and an interactive writing activity. Reading achievement accelerated to four times the growth observed in students not taking the course. All this points to the fact that it is never too late to design instruction that will benefit struggling readers.

---

struggling readers (Davidson & Koppenhaver, 1993; Showers et al., 1998; Morris et al., 1996). I know of only a single state, Wisconsin, that has historically mandated that middle schools and high schools employ certified reading teachers in reasonable numbers. Most states do not even target funds for reading teachers at these levels.

At the very least schools serving adolescents should have expert support available for students willing to seek it out. This might be in the form of a reading/writing center that operates during part of the school day and after school. I am thinking here of programs modeled after the college/university reading and writing support center. There is no mandate to attend but the center is available to students who seek support when they feel they need it. Some students might attend regularly, perhaps daily, while others would drop in whenever they were confronted with assignments that produced that panicky I-need-some-help feeling. The center might even make use of peers as tutors assuming that training on how to help is available. The center might work to foster the development of peer support and study groups for either particular types of academic needs or for particular courses or class projects. Finally, such a center might organize the training of adolescents as tutors for younger struggling readers. There is again good evidence that adolescent struggling readers benefit from tutoring younger struggling readers (and the younger readers benefit also). But both training and supervision are necessary components (Berger & Shafran, 2000; Davidson & Koppenhaver, 1993; Juel, 1994).

Other similar models emphasize voluntary reading by adolescents and their discussion of this reading with peers, who may have read the same texts (Alverman et al., 1999; Davidson & Koppenhaver, 1993). In such programs the goal is to entice adolescent readers into participating in the very activities that seem essential for their continued literacy development—more extensive reading and engagement in literate talk about books and stories and the ideas found in them. Attendance again is typically voluntary and the sessions typically are scheduled outside the normal school day. The best programs of this sort were so enticing that word-of-mouth promotion by participating adolescents produced more interested teens than could be handled given the budgets available.

I would argue that some adolescents will need something akin to the traditional "reading development class"—that is, a daily fifty-minute (or every other day 100-minute) class devoted to accelerating literacy development. Wilhelm (1998) describes the sort of instruction that I imagine would be most useful. Students are engaged in some common reading that serves as one basis for "strategy lessons"—including class conversations—but self-selected reading plays a crucial role. Often the focus, at least initially (for the year or so), is on fostering "active mental activity"—or engagement—while reading. Wilhelm notes that many of the early adolescents he worked with—students who had struggled through remedial reading and learning disability classes since the primary grades—had learned to word call but had never actually read anything if we expect "active mental activity" during reading. These students did not visualize characters or settings, they did not get goosebumps or giggle when they read, they just plowed through the words, trying to get it over with.

In an ideal world, adolescents who needed tutoring would get it. Those who needed very-small-group instruction would have such lessons daily. In both cases instruction would be provided by a teacher expert at puzzling through the problems adolescent readers and writers face. We are very far from that ideal as this book is written but if students are expected to achieve the new high standards then it seems morally incumbent that access to instruction of sufficient intensity and of sufficient expertness become routinely available to adolescent students.

In my ideal world every teacher would be a teacher of reading. Every history teacher would work to help students understand the typical structure of discourse in historical texts. They would model and demonstrate how historians think as they read and write texts. They would offer powerful instruction that fostered the development of historical vocabulary. And biology teachers would do the same sorts of things with the reading and writing expected in biology. They would help students learn to read, write, and think like biologists. In all cases content teachers would select texts for students that were well written and of appropriate levels of complexity given the students' prior knowledge as well as their levels of literacy development. If this were to happen we would experience a "win-win" outcome—students would develop not just better reading and writing skills but they would also learn more history and biology. In my view, it is neither the job of the reading or special education teacher to teach history or biology nor to find the texts that fit the students in those classes—that is rightfully the job of the history and biology teachers. But if reading and special education teachers don't help the kids struggling in those history and biology classes, who will?

Content Support.   In addition to providing literacy intervention programs, schools are going to have to rethink how content class (e.g., Global Studies, Earth Science, Algebra) support will be provided. What many content teachers view as "reading/writing problems" are actually content learning problems. When students have inadequate prior knowledge of a topic under study, for instance, they cannot make much sense of a text on that topic. Content textbooks are notoriously bad on several dimensions (try to find any study of content textbooks that offer even faint praise for middle school or high school science and social studies textbooks, for instance).

As expectations for demonstrations of greater academic learning during adolescence increase (more math courses, more science, more history courses needed to graduate), there will arise a greater need for content tutoring. Neither reading teachers nor special education teachers should be expected to reteach earth science concepts and vocabulary, for instance. Such instruction should come from content specialists, in this case, teachers with expertise in earth science. Of course, if the basic problem is that the earth science teacher selected a textbook that many students cannot read given their current level of literacy development, then tutoring is not the most direct solution to the problem that such decisions create. However, it is unlikely that many reading or special education teachers have much expertise in locating alternative, appropriately difficult earth science texts. But, again, the point is that not all students will grasp basic earth science concepts and understandings with any single set of lessons. Some will get it, some won't. Typically, failure to "get it" from the standard lesson offered has meant simply that the student failed. However, now that high schools in some states are being graded based on the number of students who pass the earth science test or course, there seems to be more interest in attempting to develop interventions that increase the numbers of passing students (or increasing the number of students who know the basics of earth science).

Thus, I see a need for middle schools and high schools to develop a second support strand: content mastery programs. Such programs might operate during the school day or in after school programs or as summer school programs (though the latter seem the most expensive and least effective option). In the high school our children attended (rated as one of the 100 best high schools in the nation by *Newsweek*), there has been an end-of-day "open" period for at least a decade. Every teacher is available every other day for small-group reteaching, review, or remediation during this period. Sports teams do not begin practices until after this period. Buses do not arrive until after this period is completed. Students can use the period as a study hall, for library work, or for a "second-shot follow-up" in any class they might be having difficulty in. This practice, in one of the nation's highest-achieving schools may offer some insight as to why it is one of the highest-achieving schools.

SUMMARY

Throughout this book I have focused on what I see as the few things that really matter for struggling readers. These few things are, I believe, as applicable to interventions targeted to adolescent populations as to elementary students. The 100/100 goal is appropriate for a K–12 system and not just applicable to a K–5 (or a K–3) school. We need to worry about how to redesign middle schools and high schools so that all students are engaged in appropriate instruction all day. At these levels the programs are necessarily focused and structured a bit differently from those targeting early grades intervention. But schools (and states) have often neglected to plan for interventions much beyond the early grades. This must change.

7

AFTERWORD

In response to an attack on the quality of American schools today, a pundit is said to have replied that "Our schools are doing pretty good at what we used to want them to do but we don't want them to do that anymore!" In many senses that simple statement does pretty much sum the current state of affairs. Average levels of reading achievement have been rising, the gap between more and less advantaged students has been narrowing, and public and political interest in education seems at an all-time high. But there have been no celebratory parades or parties.

The goals for American education have changed dramatically and probably for the better. Creating schools where all students are successful and where they all acquire quite sophisticated academic understandings and proficiencies is hard to argue against. Likewise the shift to an information economy and the dramatic shift in general information access and flow suggest that adult citizens of the future will benefit from a broad attainment of these goals. But the trick is that we will have to create a type of school that has never existed before in order to attain the new goals set for primary and secondary education. Even trickier is using the available research, almost none of which has been benchmarked against these new goals, in the design of new programs to meet these goals.

No school has ever produced students who could all read and write and do math at the Proficient Level, for instance, on the National Assessment of Educational Progress. None. That we don't have such schools suggests the enormity of the tasks ahead. It may be possible to create such schools but there is little research that suggests just what those schools should look like. Too often, in my view, school reform research that was never benchmarked against attainment of the new standards is being touted as providing the needed guidance. Perhaps. But what would be truly useful is research on schools where the new standards are being successfully met. For that though we will have to wait. Thus, in my view much of the criticism of current school programs is unwarranted, many of the popular solutions untested against the new goals, such that much of the evangelical promotion of favorite programs is misguided at best and simply profit-oriented at worst.

Research-Based Advice
versus Commercial Advocacy and Advertising

Jere Brophy (2000), award-winning researcher and classroom scholar has recently noted:

> Teachers are rightly confused and irritated by the seemingly continuous shifts and contradictions in the advice directed at them by supposed experts. However, I will submit that the problem is not being caused by researchers.... Researchers stay close to their data and make careful, qualified statements about implications. The kinds of overblown, polarized, and evangelical statements that cause most of the problems are coming not from researchers but from people whose policy advocacy is based on strong theoretical biases and who typically have something to sell but little or no scientific support for their claims and recommendations. (p. 177)

I wish I could tell you that the ideas and strategies sketched in this book will turn the tide and that then all will be well in America. They won't. I do hope that they will help set us on a course more likely to lead us where we need to go. In fact, if I wasn't confident that the evidence on high-achieving schools and classrooms now available pointed to these ideas and strategies as reasonable directions for our work, I wouldn't have bothered to write this small book.

For those readers hoping for a step-by-step manual for school reform, I'm sorry to have disappointed you. My basic goal has been to push all of us toward thinking more about those things that a century's worth of research and experimentation have indicated are the best bets for helping us in creating those schools we do not have. Developing the instructional expertise of every teacher, reorganizing schools so that supporting teacher development is, as they say, Job Number 1, is the only strategy that I can endorse with any enthusiasm and the only one that I can find substantial research support for.

For those who hoped for more advice on early intervention (preschool through first grade) I have suggested a number of other available resources throughout the book. As I noted in the *Foreword*, the emphasis on early intervention has generated a plethora of books, materials, and programs from which to review and draw ideas. I will humbly suggest that the key principles set out in this book are also critically important in early literacy instruction. But it is grade 2 and beyond that has been much neglected in the advice offered for improving literacy proficiency. Thus, it is those grades that have been my focus in this book. While the issues of phonemic awareness and phonics have generated a plethora of papers, books, and materials, the critical topics of fluency and comprehension strategy development have fostered much less interest. Thus, I focused my attention on them. Finally, as governors, presidents, and politicians, generally, have begun to recommend after-school and summer school programs as one way to meet the challenge of struggling readers, research and demonstration efforts have lagged behind. Thus, I have attempted to summarize what we know about effective reading instructional designs in the hopes that students will spend this extra instructional time profitably.

I will close by reiterating the advice that Pat Cunningham and I offered in *Schools That Work* (one of the four books in this series): Think long and move slowly but always move forward. By this I mean, think about what you want to see happening in your school three to five years from now and begin working to get there. Change is hard. Change is anxiety-provoking and necessarily slow. My own experience suggests that when we try to change everything at once, little that matters actually changes. But someone has to initiate and support the needed change. If not you, who will? If not today, when?

Finally, remember that in the end it will still be teachers who make the difference in children's school lives. It is teachers who will either lead the change or resist and stymie it. The focus of school change has to be on supporting teachers in their efforts to become more expert and reorganizing all the aspects of the educational system so that they can teach as expertly as they know how. But bureaucracies rarely give up power easily and they rarely seem to improve people. In my most optimistic moments I believe that people can change bureaucracies in positive ways. I hope that this book provides some of you with the confidence necessary to challenge bureaucratic nonsense when it arrives at your doorstep. No one knows your students as well as you do and no one knows their needs better. In the end, it is unlikely that anyone else in the bureaucracy cares more about your students than you. So fight for them when you must. Fight for the resources to create classrooms that meet, or come close to meeting the 100/100 goal. The closer we come to achieving that goal the closer we will be to providing what really matters for struggling readers.

BIBLIOGRAPHY

Achilles, C. M. (1999). *Let's Put Kids First, Finally: Getting Class Size Right.* Thousand Oaks, CA: Corwin Press.

Adams, G. L., & Englemann, S. (1996). *Research on direct instruction: Twenty-five years beyond DISTAR.* Eugene, OR: Educational Achievement Systems.

Allington, R. L. (1977). "If They Don't Read Much, How They Ever Gonna Get Good?" *Journal of Reading, 21,* 57–61.

——, (1980). "Poor Readers Don't Get to Read Much in Reading Groups." *Language Arts, 57,* 872–877.

——, (1980). "Teacher Interruption Behaviors During Primary Grade Oral Reading." *Journal of Educational Psychology, 72,* 371–377.

——, (1983). "Fluency: The Neglected Goal." *Reading Teacher, 36,* 556–561.

——, (1983). "The Reading Instruction Provided Readers of Differing Abilities." *Elementary School Journal, 83,* 548–559.

——, (1984). "Content Coverage and Contextual Reading in Reading Groups." *Journal of Reading Behavior, 16,* 85–96.

——, (1984). "Oral Reading." In P. D. Pearson (ed.), *Handbook of Reading Research* (pp. 829–864). New York: Longman.

——, (1987). "Shattered Hopes: Why Two Federal Programs Have Failed to Correct Reading Failure." *Learning, 13,* 60–64.

——, (1991). "The Legacy of 'Slow It Down and Make It More Concrete.'" In J. Zuten & S. McCormick (eds.), *Learner Factors/Teacher Factors: Issues in Literacy Research and Instruction* (40th Yearbook of the National Reading Conference, pp. 19–30). Chicago: National Reading Conference.

——, (1994). "The Schools We Have. The Schools We Need." *Reading Teacher, 48,* 2–16.

——, (2001). "Research on Reading/Learning Disability Interventions." In S. J. Samuels & A. Farstrup (eds.), *What Research Says about Reading Instruction.* Newark, DE: International Reading Association.

——, & Cunningham, P. M. (2001). *Schools That Work: Where All Children Read and Write,* 2nd ed. New York: Longman.

——, Guice, S., Michaelson, N., Baker, K., and Li, S. (1996). "Literature-Based Curriculum in High-Poverty Schools." In M. Graves, P. v. d. Broek, & B. Taylor (eds.), *The First R: Every Child's Right to Read* (pp. 73–96). New York: Teachers College Press.

——, & Johnston, P. (April 2000). *Exemplary Fourth-Grade Reading Instruction.* Paper presented at the American Educational Research Association, New Orleans.

——— & McGill-Franzen, A. (1989). "School Response to Reading Failure: Chapter 1 and Special Education Students in Grades 2, 4, and 8." *Elementary School Journal, 89*, 529–542.

———, & McGill-Franzen, A. (1996). "Individual Planning." In M. Wang & M. Reynolds (eds.), *Handbook of Special and Remedial Education* (pp. 5–35). New York: Pergamon.

———, & Walmsley, S. A. (1995). *No Quick Fix: Rethinking Literacy Programs in American Elementary Schools.* New York: Teachers College Press.

———, & Woodside-Jiron, H. (1998). "Thirty Years of Research...: When Is a Research Summary Not a Research Summary?" In K. Goodman (ed.), *In defense of good teaching: What Teachers Need to Know about the Reading Wars* (pp. 143–157). York, ME: Stenhouse.

———, & Woodside-Jiron, H. (1999). "The Politics of Literacy Teaching: How 'Research' Shaped Educational Policy." *Educational Researcher, 28*(8), 4–13.

Alvermann, D. E., Young, J. P., Green, C., & Wisenbaker, J. M. (1999). "Adolescents' Perceptions and Negotiations of Literacy Practices in After-School Read and Talk Clubs." *American Educational Research Journal, 36*(2), 221–264.

Anderson, R. C., Wilson, P., & Fielding, L. (1988). "Growth in Reading and How Children Spend Their Time Outside of School." *Reading Research Quarterly, 23*(3), 285–303.

Anderson, V., & Roit, M. (1993). "Planning and Implementing Collaborative Strategy Instruction for Delayed Readers in Grades 6–10." *Elementary School Journal, 94*, 121–137.

Applebee, A. N. (1991). "Literature: Whose Heritage?" In E. Hiebert (ed.), *Literacy for a Diverse Society: Perspective, Practices, and Policies.* New York: Teachers College Press.

Au, K., & Jordan, C. (1980). "Teaching Reading to Hawaiian Children: Finding a Culturally Appropriate Solution." In H. T. Trueba, G. P. Guthrie, & K. Au (eds.), *Culture and the Bilingual Classroom* (pp. 139–152). Rowley, MA: Newbury House.

Baumann, J. F., & Duffy, A. M. (1997). *Engaged Reading for Pleasure and Learning.* Athens, GA: National Reading Research Center, University of Georgia.

Bembry, K. L., Jordan, H. R., Gomez, E., Anderson, M., & Mendro, R. L. (1998). *Policy Implications of Long-Term Teacher Effects on Student Achievement.* Paper presented at the American Educational Research Association.

Beck, I. L., McKeown, M. G., Hamilton, R. L., & Kucan, L. (1997). *Questioning the Author.* Newark, DE: International Reading Association.

Berger, A., & Shafran, E. (2000). *Teens for Literacy.* Newark, DE: International Reading Association.

Bergman, J. L. (1992). "SAIL—A Way to Success and Independence for Low-Achieving Readers." *Reading Teacher, 45*, 598–603.

Berliner, D. C. (1981). "Academic Learning Time and Reading Achievement." In J. Guthrie (ed.), *Comprehension and Teaching: Research Reviews* (pp. 203–225). Newark, DE: International Reading Association.

———, & Biddle, B. (1995). *The Manufactured Crisis.* New York: Longman.

Betts, E. A. (1946). *Foundations of Reading Instruction.* New York: American Book Co.

Biemiller, A. (1970). "The Development of the Use of Graphic and Contextual Information as Children Learn to Read." *Reading Research Quarterly* , *6*, 75–96.

Binkley, M., & Williams, T. (1996). *Reading Literacy in the United States: Findings from the IEA Reading Literacy Study* (NCES 96–258). Washington, DC: U.S. Department of Education, Office of Educational Research and Improvement.

Block, C. C. (1993). "Strategy Instruction in a Literature-Based Program." *Elementary School Journal, 94*, 139–151.

Block, J. H. (1980). "Success Rate." In C. Denham & A. Lieberman (eds.), *Time to Learn*. Washington, DC: National Institute of Education.

Bond, G. L., & Dykstra, R. (1967). "The Cooperative Research Program in First-Grade Reading Instruction." *Reading Research Quarterly, 2*(4), 5–142.

Boyd-Zaharias, J., & Pate-Bain, H. (1998). *Teacher Aides and Student Learning: Lessons from Project STAR*. Arlington, VA: Educational Research Service.

Bracey, G. W. (1997). *Setting the Record Straight: Responses to Misconceptions about Public Education in the United States*. Alexandria, VA: Association for Supervision and Curriculum Development.

Brandt, R. (October 1986). "On the Expert Teacher: A Conversation with David Berliner." *Educational Leadership, 44*, 4–9.

Brophy, J. (2000). "Beyond Balance: Goal Awareness, Developmental Progressions, Tailoring to the Context, and Supports for Teachers in Ideal Reading and Literacy Programs." In M. Graves, P. van den Broek, B. Taylor (ed.), *Reading for Meaning: Fostering Comprehension in the Middle Grades* (pp. 170–192). New York: Teachers College Press.

Brown, R. G. (1991). *Schools of Thought: How the Politics of Literacy Shape Thinking in the Classroom*. San Francisco: Jossey-Bass.

Bruer, J. T. (1994). *Schools for Thought: A Science for Learning in the Classroom*. Cambridge, MA: MIT Press.

Carpenter, R., & Pearson, P. D. (December 1999). *Estimating Summer School Reading Achievement*. Paper presented at the National Reading Conference, Austin, TX.

Carter, L. (1984). "The Sustaining Effects Study of Compensatory and Elementary Education." *Educational Researcher, 12*, 4–13.

Cazden, C. B. (1988). *Classroom Discourse: The Language of Teaching and Learning*. Portsmouth, NH: Heinemenn.

Chall, J. S. (1983). *Stages of Reading Development*. New York, NY: McGraw-Hill.

——, & Dale, E. (1995). *The Dale-Chall Readability Formula*. Brookline, MA: Brookline Books.

——, (1987). *Learning to Read: The Great Debate*. (Updated ed.) New York: McGraw-Hill.

——, Bissex, G., Conard, S., and Harris-Sharples, S. (1996). *Qualitative Assessment of Text Difficulty: A Practical Guide for Teachers and Authors*. Cambridge, MA: Brookline.

——, & Conard, S. S. (1991). *Should Textbooks Challenge Students?* New York: Teachers College Press.

Chinn, C. A., Waggoner, M. A., Anderson, R. C., Schommer, M., & Wilkinson, I. (1993). "Situated Actions During Reading Lessons: A Microanalysis of

Oral Reading Error Episodes." *American Educational Research Journal, 30,* 361–392.

Chomsky, C. (1972). "Stages in Language Development and Reading Exposure." *Harvard Educational Review, 42,* 1–33.

Cipielewski, J., & Stanovich, K. (1992). "Predicting Growth in Reading Ability from Children's Exposure to Print." *Journal of Experimental Child Psychology, 54,* 74–89.

Clay, M. M. (1993). *An observation survey of early literacy achievement.* Portsmouth, NH: Heinemann.

———, & Imlach, R. H. (1971). "Juncture, Pitch, and Stress as Reading Behavior Variables." *Journal of Verbal Learning and Verbal Behavior, 10,* 133–139.

Coles, G. (1998). *Reading Lessons: The Debate Over Literacy.* New York: Hill & Wang.

———. (2000). *Misreading Reading.* Portsmouth, NH: Heinemann.

Collins, C. (1991). Reading instruction that increases thinking abilities. *Journal of Reading, 34,* 510–516.

Collins, J. (1986). "Differential Instruction in Reading Groups." In J. Cook-Gumperz (ed.), *The Social Construction of Literacy* (pp. 117–137). New York: Cambridge University Press.

Cooper, H., Nye, B., Charlton, K., Lindsay, J., & Greathouse, S. (1996). "The Effects of Summer Vacation on Achievement Test Scores: A Narrative and Meta-Analytic Review." *Review of Educational Research, 66* (3, Fall), 227–268.

Cuban, L. (1993). *How Teachers Taught: Constancy and Change in American Classrooms, 1880–1990,* 2nd ed. New York: Longman.

Cunningham, A. E., & Stanovich, K. E. (1998). "The Impact of Print Exposure on Word Recognition." In J. Metsala & L. Ehri (eds.), *Word Recognition in Beginning Literacy* (pp. 235–262). Mahwah, NJ: Lawrence Erlbaum Associates.

Cunningham, P. M. (2000). *Phonics They Use: Words for Reading and Writing.* 3rd ed. New York: Longman.

———, & Allington, R. L. (1999). *Classrooms that Work: They Can All Read and Write,* 2nd ed. New York: Longman.

Dahl, K. L., & Freppon, P. A. (1995). "A Comparison of Inner-City Children's Interpretations of Reading and Writing Instruction in Skills-Based and Whole Language Classrooms. *Reading Research Quarterly, 30,* 50–74.

Dahl, P. R. (1977). "An Experimental Program for Teaching High-Speed Word Recognition and Comprehension Skills." In J. Button, T. Lovitt, & T. Rowland (eds.), *Communications Research in Learning Disabilities and Mental Retardation.* Baltimore: University Park Press.

Darling-Hammond, L. (1990). "Instructional Policy into Practice: 'The Power of the Bottom Over the Top.'" *Educational Evaluation and Policy Analysis, 12* (3), 233–241.

Darling-Hammond, L. (1997). *Doing What Matters Most: Investing in Quality Teaching.* National Commission on Teaching and America's Future. New York: NY.

———. (1998). "Teachers and Teaching: Testing Policy Hypotheses from a National Commission Report." *Educational Researcher, 27*(1), 5–15.

Davidson, J., & Koppenhaver, D. (1993). *Adolescent Literacy: What Works and Why*, 2nd ed. Hamden, CT: Garland Publishing.

Delpit, L. (1995). *Other People's Children: Cultural Conflict in the Classroom*. New York: The Free Press.

Denham, C., & Lieberman, A. (1980). *Time to Learn*. Washington, DC: U.S. Government Printing Office (1980-695-717).

Dickinson, D. K., & Smith, M. W. (1994). "Long-Term Effects of Preschool Teachers' Book Readings on Low-Income Children's Vocabulary and Story Comprehension." *Reading Research Quarterly*, 29(2), 104–123.

Dole, J., Brown, K. J., & Trathen, W. (1996). "The Effects of Strategy Instruction on the Comprehension Performance of At-Risk Students." *Reading Research Quarterly*, 31(1), 62–88.

Donahue, P. L., Voelkl, K. E., Campbell, J. R., & Mazzeo, J. (1999). *NAEP 1998 Reading Report Card for the Nation and the States*. (NCES 1999–500). National Center for Education Statistics, Office of Educational Research and Improvement, U.S. Department of Education.

Dowhower, S. L. (1987). "Effects of Repeated Reading on Second Grade Transitional Readers' Fluency and Comprehension." *Reading Research Quarterly*, 22, 389–406.

Doyle, W. (1983). "Academic Work." *Review of Educational Research*, 53, 159–199.

Duffy, G. G. (1993). "Teachers' Progress Toward Becoming Expert Strategy Teachers." *Elementary School Journal*, 94(2), 109–120.

———, & Hoffman, J. V. (1999). "In Pursuit of an Illusion: The Search for a Perfect Method." *Reading Teacher*, 53(1), 10–16.

———, Roehler, L., & Rackliffe, G. (1986). "How Teachers' Instructional Talk Influences Student Understanding of Lesson Content." *Elementary School Journal*, 87, 3–16.

Duffy-Hester, A. (1999). "Teaching Struggling Readers in Elementary School Classrooms: A Review of Classroom Reading Programs and Principles for Instruction." *Reading Teacher*, 52(5), 480–495.

Duthie, C. (1996). *True Stories: Nonfiction in the Primary Classroom*. York, ME: Stenhouse.

Dweck, C. S. (1999). *Self-Theories: Their Role in Motivation, Personality, and Development*. Philadephia: Taylor & Francis.

Egoff, S. (1972). "If That Don't Do No Good, That Won't Do No Harm: The Uses and Dangers of Mediocrity in Children's Reading." *School Library Journal* (October).

Eldredge, J. L., Reutzel, D. R., & Hollingsworth, P. M. (1996). "Comparing the Effectiveness of Two Oral Reading Practices: Round-Robin Reading and the Shared Book Experience." *Journal of Literacy Research*, 28(2), 201–225.

Elley, W. B. (1992). *How in the World Do Students Read? IEA Study of Reading Literacy*. The Hague, Netherlands: International Association for the Evaluation of Educational Achievement.

Elmore, R. F., Peterson, P. L., & McCarthy, S. J. (1996). *Restructuring in the Classroom: Teaching, Learning, and School Organization*. San Francisco: Jossey-Bass.

Entwisle, D. R., Alexander, K. L., & Olson, L. S. (1997). *Children, Schools, and Inequality*. Boulder, CO: Westview Press.

Ferguson, R. F. (1991). "Paying for Public Education: New Evidence on How and Why Money Matters." *Harvard Journal on Legislation, 28*, 465–491.

Fisher, C. W., & Berliner, D. C. (1985). *Perspectives on Instructional Time*. New York: Longman.

Foertsch, M. A. (1992). *Reading In and Out of School: Achievement of American Students in Grades 4, 8, and 12 in 1989–90*. Washington, DC: National Center for Educational Statistics: U.S. Government Printing Office.

Fountas, I. C., & Pinnell, G. S. (1999). *Matching Books to Readers: Using Leveled Books in Guided Reading, K–3*. Portsmouth, NH: Heinemann.

Gambrell, L. B., & Marinak, B. A. (1997). "Incentives and Intrinsic Motivation to Read." In J. T. Guthrie & A. Wigfield (eds.), *Reading Engagement: Motivating Readers Through Integrated Instruction.* (pp. 205–216). Newark, DE: International Reading Association.

———, Wilson, R. M., & Gantt, W. N. (1981). "Classroom Observations of Task-Attending Behaviors of Good and Poor Readers." *Journal of Educational Research, 74*(6), 400–404.

Gaskins, I. W., & Elliot, T. T. (1991). *Implementing Cognitive Strategy Instruction Across the School: The Benchmark Manual for Teachers*. Cambridge, MA: Brookline.

Gaskins, R. W. (1996). "'That's Just How It Was': The Effect of Issue Related Emotional Involvement on Reading Comprehension." *Reading Research Quarterly, 31*, 386–405.

Glass, G. V. (1983). "Effectiveness of Special Education." *Policy Studies Review, 2*, 65–78.

Goatley, V. J., Brock, C. H., & Raphael, T. E. (1995). "Diverse Learners Participating in Regular Education 'Book Clubs.'" *Reading Research Quarterly, 30*(3), 352–380.

Goodlad, J. I. (1983). *A Place Called School: Prospects for the Future*. New York: McGraw-Hill.

Grissmer, D. W., Kirby, S. N., Berends, M., & Williamson, S. (1994). *Student Achievement and the Changing American Family*. Santa Monica, CA: RAND: Institute on Education and Training.

Guice, S., Allington, R. L., Johnston, P., Baker, K., & Michelson, N. (1996). "Access?: Books, Children, and Literature-Based Curriculum in Schools." *The New Advocate, 9*(3), 197–207.

Guthrie, J. T., & Anderson, E. (1999). "Engagement in Reading: Processes of Motivated, Strategic, Knowledgeable, Social Readers." In J. T. Guthrie & D. Alvermann (eds.), *Engaged Reading: Processes, Practices, and Policy Implications* (pp. 17–45). New York: Teachers College.

———, Van Meter, P., McCann, A., Wigfield, A., Bennett, I., Poundstone, C., Rice, M., Faibisch, F., Hunt, B., & Mitchell, A. (1996). "Growth of Literacy Engagement: Changes in Motivations and Strategies During Concept-Oriented Reading Instruction." *Reading Research Quarterly, 31*, 306–322.

Guthrie, J. T., Wigfield, A., Metsala, J., & Cox, K. (1999). "Motivational and Cognitive Predictors of Text Comprehension and Reading Amount." *Scientific Studies of Reading, 3*(3), 231–256.

Halpern, R. (1999). "After-School Programs for Low-Income Children: Promise and Challenges." *The Future of Children*, 9(2), 81–95.

Harris, A. J., & Sipay, E. R. (1990). *How to Increase Reading Ability*, 8th ed. New York, NY: Longman.

Harvey, S., & Goudvis, A. (2000). *Strategies that Work: Teaching Comprehension to Enhance Understanding*. York, ME: Stenhouse.

Haynes, M. C. & Jenkins, J. R. (1986). "Reading Instruction in Special Education Resource Rooms." *American Educational Research Journal*, 23(2), 161–190.

Herman, P. (1985). "The Effect of Repeated Readings on Reading Rate, Speech Pauses, and Word Recognition Accuracy." *Reading Research Quarterly*, 20, 553–565.

Hiebert, E. H. (1983). "An Examination of Ability Grouping for Reading Instruction", *Reading Research Quarterly*, 18, 231–255.

Hoffman, J. V., O'Neal, S. F., Kastler, L., Clements, R., Segel, K., & Nash, M. (1984). "Guided Oral Reading and Miscue Focused Verbal Feedback in Second Grade Classrooms." *Reading Research Quarterly*, 19, 367–384.

———, McCarthy, S. J., Elliott, B., Bayles, D., Price, D., Ferree, A., & Abbott, J. (1998). "The Literature-Based Basals in First-Grade Classrooms: Savior, Satan, or Same-Old, Same-Old?" *Reading Research Quarterly*, 33(2), 168–197.

Holdaway, D. (1979). *The Foundations of Literacy*. Sydney, Australia: Ashton-Scholastic.

House, E. R. (1991). "Big Policy, Little Policy." *Educational Researcher*, 20, 21–26.

———, Glass, G. V., McLean, L. & Walker, D. (1978). "No Simple Answers: Critique of the Follow Through Evaluation." *Harvard Educational Review*, 48, 128–160.

Invernizzi, M., Rosemary, C., Juel, C., & Richards, H. (1997). "At-Risk Readers and Community Volunteers: A Three-Year Perspective." *Scientific Studies of Reading*, 1(3), 277–300.

Ivey, G. (1999). "A Multicase Study in the Middle School: Complexities Among Young Adolescent Readers." *Reading Research Quarterly*, 34, 172–193.

Jenkins, C. B. (1999). *The Allure of Authors: Author Studies in the Elementary Classroom*. Portsmouth, NH: Heinemann.

Johnston, P. (1985). "Understanding Reading Failure: A Case Study Approach." *Harvard Educational Review*, 55(2), 153–177.

———, & Allington, R. L. (1991). Remediation. In P. D. Pearson (ed.), *Handbook of Reading Research, Vol. II* (pp. 984–1012). New York: Longman.

———, Allington, R. L., Guice, S., & Brooks, G. W. (1998). "Small Change: A Multi-Level Study of the Implementation of Literature-Based Instruction." *Peabody Journal of Education*, 73(3), 81–103.

Juel, C. (1994). *Learning to Read and Write in One Elementary School*. New York: Springer-Verlag.

——— (1996). "What Makes Literacy Tutoring Effective?" *Reading Research Quarterly*, 31(3), 268–289.

Keene, E. O., & Zimmerman, S. (1997). *Mosaic of Thought: Teaching Comprehension in a Reader's Workshop*. Portsmouth, NH: Heinemann.

Kibby, M. W. (1995). *Student Literacy: Myths and Realities* (Fastback 381). Bloomington, IN: Phi Delta Kappa Educational Foundation.

Keisling, H. (1978). "Productivity of Instructional Time by Mode of Instruction for Students at Varying Levels of Reading Skill. *Reading Research Quarterly, 13,* 554–582.

Klare, G. R. (1984). "Readability." In P. D. Pearson (ed.), *Handbook of Reading Research* (pp. 681–744). New York: Longman.

Knapp, M. S. (1995). *Teaching for Meaning in High-Poverty Classrooms.* New York: Teachers College Press.

Kos, R. (1991). "Persistence of Reading Disabilities: Voices of Four Middle-School Students." *American Educational Research Journal, 28,* 875–895.

Koslin, B. l., Zeno, S., & Koslin, S. (1987). *The DRP: An Effective Measure in Reading.* New York: College Entrance Examination Board.

Kozol, J. (1991). *Savage Inequalities: Children in America's Schools.* New York: Crown.

Krashen, S. (1993). *The Power of Reading: Insights from the Research.* Englewood, CO: Libraries Unlimited.

Kucan, L., & Beck, I. L. (1997). "Thinking Aloud and Reading Comprehension Research: Inquiry, Instruction, and Social Interaction." *Review of Educational Research, 67*(3), 271–299.

LaBerge, D., & Samuels, S. J. (1974). "Toward a Theory of Automatic Information Processing in Reading." *Cognitive Psychology, 6,* 293–323.

Langer, J. A. (1995). *Envisioning Literature: Literary Understanding and Literature Instruction.* New York: Teachers College Press.

Leinhardt, G., & Pallay, A. (1982). Restrictive Educational Settings: Exile or Haven?" *Review of Educational Research, 52*(4), 557–578.

———, Zigmond, N., & Cooley, W. (1981). "Reading Instruction and Its Effects." *American Educational Research Journal, 18*(3), 343–361.

Lyon, G. R., & Moats, L. C. (1997). "Critical Conceptual and Methodological Considerations in Reading Intervention Research." *Journal of Learning Disabilities, 30*(6), 578–588.

Lysynchuk, L. M., Pressley, M., D'Ailly, H., Smith, M., & Cake, H. (1989). "A Methodological Analysis of Experimental Studies of Comprehension Strategy Instruction." *Reading Research Quarterly, 24,* 458–470.

Mace, A. (1997). "Organizing the Instructional Resource Room." In M. Herzog (ed.), *Inside Learning Network Schools.* Katonah, NY: Richard C. Owen.

Mastropieri, M. A., & Scruggs, T. E. (1997). "Best Practices in Promoting Reading Comprehension in Students with Learning Disabilities, 1976–1996." *Remedial and Special Education, 18*(4), 197–213.

McBride-Chang, C., Manis, F., Seidenberg, M., Custodio, R., & Doi, L. (1993). "Print Exposure as a Predictor of Word Reading and Reading Comprehension in Disabled and Nondisabled Readers." *Journal of Educational Psychology, 85,* 230–238.

McGill-Franzen, A. (1993). "'I Could Read the Words!': Selecting Good Books for Inexperienced Readers." *Reading Teacher, 46*(6), 424–426.

———. (1996). "Three Children, Three Stories of School and Literacy." *Language and Literacy Spectrum, 6,* 45–51.

———, & Allington, R. L. (1990). "Comprehension and Coherence: Neglected Elements of Literacy Instruction in Remedial and Resource Room Services." *Journal of Reading, Writing, and Learning Disabilities, 6,* 149–182.

———, Allington, R. L., Yokoi, L., & Brooks, G. (1999). "Putting Books in the Room Seems Necessary but Not Sufficient." *Journal of Educational Research, 93*(2), 67–74.

———, Ward, N., Goatley, V., & Machado, V. (2000). *Teachers' Use of the New Standards Frameworks and Assessments in English Language Arts and Social Studies: Local Cases of New York State Elementary Grade Teachers.* National Research Center on English Learning and Achievement: University at Albany-SUNY.

———, & Lanford, C. (1994). "Exposing the Edge of the Preschool Curriculum: Teachers' Talk about Text and Children's Literary Understandings." *Language Arts, 71,* 264–273.

McQuillan, J. (1998). *The Literacy Crisis: False Claims, Real Solutions.* Portsmouth, NH: Heinemann.

Mervar, K., & Hiebert, E. H. (1989). "Literature-Selection Strategies and Amount of Reading in Two Literacy Approaches." In S. McCormick & J. Zutell (eds.), *Cognitive and Social Perspectives for Literacy Research and Instruction* (pp. 529–535). Chicago: NRC.

Morris, D., Ervin, C., & Conrad, K. (1996). "A Case Study of Middle School Reading Disability." *Reading Teacher, 49,* 368–377.

Morrow, L. M. (1992). "The Impact of a Literature-Based Program on Literacy Achievement, Use of Literature, and Attitudes of Children from Minority Backgrounds." *Reading Research Quarterly, 27*(3), 250–275.

———, Pressley, M., Smith, J., & Smith, M. (1997). "The Effect of a Literature-Based Integrated into Literacy and Science Instruction with Children from Diverse Backgrounds." *Reading Research Quarterly, 32*(1), 54–76.

Nagy, W., & Anderson, R. C. (1984). "How Many Words are There in Printed School English?" *Reading Research Quarterly, 19,* 304–330.

Nystrand, M., Gamoran, A., Kachur, R., & Prendergast, C. (1997). *Opening Dialogue: Understanding the Dynamics of Language and Learning in the English Classroom.* New York: Teachers College Press.

Ohanian, S. (1999). *One Size Fits Few.* Portsmouth, NH: Heinemann.

O'Shea, L. J., Sindelar, P. T., & O'Shea, D. J. (1985). "The Effects of Repeated Reading and Attentional Cues on Reading Fluency and Comprehension." *Journal of Reading Behavior, 17,* 129–146.

O'Sullivan, P. J., Ysseldyke, J. E., Christenson, S. L., & Thurlow, M. L. (1990). "Mildly Handicapped Elementary Students' Opportunity to Learn During Reading Instruction in Mainstream and Special Education Settings." *Reading Research Quarterly, 25* (#2), 131–146.

Palincsar, A. S., & Brown, A. (1984). "Reciprocal Teaching and Comprehension-Fostering and Comprehension-Monitoring Activities." *Cognition and Instruction, 1*(2), 117–175.

Paratore, J., Garnick, S., & Lewis, T. (1997). "Watching Teachers Watch Children Talk About Books." In J. Paratore & R. McCormack (eds.), *Peer Talk in the*

Classroom: Learning from the Research (pp. 207–229). Newark, DE: International Reading Association.

Pearson, P. D. (1993). "Teaching and Learning to Read: A Research Perspective." *Language Arts, 70* (502–511).

———, & Dole, J. (1987). "Explicit Comprehension Instruction: A Review of the Research and a New Conceptualization of Instruction." *Elementary School Journal, 88,* 151–165.

———, & Fielding, L. (1991). "Comprehension Instruction." In M. Kamil, R. Barr, P. Mosenthal, & P. D. Pearson (eds.), *Handbook of Reading Research, vol. 2* (pp. 815–860). New York: Longman.

Pogrow, S. (1990). "Challenging At-Risk Students: Findings from the HOTS Program." *Phi Delta Kappan, 71,* 389–397.

———, (1993). "Where's the Beef? Looking for Exemplary Materials." *Educational Leadership, 50,* 39–45.

Pressley, M. & Allington, R. L. (1999). "What Should Educational Research Be the Research Of?" *Issues in Education: Contributions from Educational Psychology, 5*(1), 1–35.

———, Johnson, C. J., Symons, S., McGoldrick, J., & Kurita, J. (1990). "Strategies That Improve Memory and Comprehension of What is Read." *Elementary School Journal, 90,* 3–32.

———, El-Dinary, P. B., Gaskins, I., Schuder, T., Bergman, J., Almasi, L., & Brown, R. (1992). "Beyond Direct Explanation: Transactional Instruction in Reading Comprehension Strategies." *Elementary School Journal, 92,* 511–554.

———, Wharton-McDonald, R., Allington, R. L., Block, C. C., Morrow, L., Tracey, D., Baker, K., Brooks, G., Cronin, J., Nelson, E., & Woo, D. (2000). "A Study of Effective First-Grade Reading Instruction." *Scientific Studies of Reading.*

Puma, M. J., Karweit, N., Price, C., Ricciuti, A., Thompson, W., & Vaden-Kiernan, M. (1997). *Prospects: Final Report on Student Outcomes.* Washington, DC: U.S. Department of Education, Planning and Evaluation Services.

Purcell-Gates, V., McIntyre, E., & Freppon, P. (1995). "Learning Written Storybook Language in School." *American Educational Research Journal, 32*(3), 659–685.

Rashotte, C., & Torgeson, J. (1985). "Repeated Readings and Reading Fluency in Learning Disabled Children." *Reading Research Quarterly, 20,* 180–189.

Rasinski, T. V. (1990). "Effects of Repeated Readings and Listening While Reading on Reading Fluency." *Journal of Educational Research, 83,* 147–150.

———. (2000). "Speed Does Matter in Reading." *Reading Teacher, 54.*

Reutzel, D. R., Hollingsworth, P. M., & Eldredge, J. L. (1994). "Oral Reading Instruction: The Impact on Student Reading Development." *Reading Research Quarterly, 29*(1), 40–65.

Richardson, V. (Ed.). (1994). *Teacher Change and the Staff Development Process: A Case in Reading Instruction.* New York: Teachers College Press.

Robinson, C. C., Larsen, J. M., & Haupt, J. H. (1996). "The Influence of Selecting and Taking Picture Books Home on the At-Home Reading Behaviors of Kindergarten Children." *Reading Research and Instruction, 35*(3), 249–259.

Rosenshine, B., & Meister, C. (1994). "Reciprocal Teaching: A Review of the Research." *Review of Educational Research, 64*(4), 479–530.

Rothstein, R. (1998a). *The Way We Were? The Myths and Realities of Ameica's Student Achievement.* New York: The Century Foundation Press.

Rowan, B., & Guthrie, L. F. (1989). "The Quality of Chapter I Instruction: Results from a Study of Twenty-Four Schools." In R. E. Slavin, N. Karweit, & N. Madden (eds.), *Effective Programs for Students at Risk* (pp. 195–219). Boston: Allyn-Bacon.

Ruddell, R. B., Draheim, M. E., & Barnes, J. (1990). "A Comparative Study of the Teaching Effectiveness of Influential and Noninfluential Teachers and Reading Comprehension Development." In J. Zutell & S. MCormick (eds.), *Literacy Theory and Research: Analyses from Multiple Paradigms* (pp. 153–162). Chicago: National Reading Conference.

Samuels, S. J., Schermer, N., & Reinking, D. (1992). "Reading Fluency: Techniques for Making Decoding Automatic." In S. J. Samuels & A. Farstrup (eds.), *What Research Has to Say about Reading Instruction* (pp. 124–144). Newark, DE: International Reading Association.

Scharer, P. L. (1992). "Teachers in Transitions: An Exploration of Changes in Teachers and Classrooms During the Implementation of Literature-Based Reading Instruction." *Research in the Teaching of English, 26* (#4, December), 408–443.

Schrieber, P. A. (1980). "On the Acquisition of Reading Fluency." *Journal of Reading Behavior, 12,* 177–186.

Schweinhart, L. J., & Weikart, D. P. (1998). "Why Curriculum Matters in Early Childhood Education." *Educational Leadership, 55* (March), 57–60.

Seppanen, P. S., Love, J. M., deVries, D. K., & Bernstein, L. (1993). *National Study of Before- and After-school Programs.* Washington, DC: U.S. Department of Education, Office of Policy and Planning.

Shanklin, N. L. (1990). "Improving the Comprehension of At-Risk Readers: An Ethnographic Study of Four Chapter 1 Teachers, Grades 4–6." *International Journal of Reading, Writing, and Learning Disabilities, 6*(2), 137–148.

Share, D. L., & Stanovich, K. E. (1995). "Cognitive Processes in Early Reading Development: Accomodating Individual Differences in a Model of Acquisition." *Issue in Education, 1*(1), 1–57.

Shepard, L. A., & Smith, M. L. (eds.). (1989). *Flunking Grades: Research and Policies on Retention.* Philadelphia: Falmer.

Showers, B., Joyce, B., Scanlon, M., & Schnaubelt, C. (March, 1998). "A Second Chance to Learn to Read." *Educational Leadership, 72,* 27–30.

Slavin, R. E., Madden, N. A., Dolan, l. J., & Wasik, B. A. (1996). *Every Child, Every School: Success for All.* Thousand Oaks, CA: Corwin.

——, Madden, N. A., Karweit, B. L., Dolan, L. J. & Wasik, B. A. (1993). "Success for All: A Comprehensive Approach to Prevention and Early Intervention." In R. E. Slavin, Karweit, B. L. & Wasik, B. A (eds.), *Preventing Early School Failure: Research, Policy and Practice* (pp. 175–205). Boston: Allyn & Bacon.

Smith, C., Constantino, R., & Krashen, S. (1997). "Differences in Print Environment: Children in Beverly Hills, Compton and Watts." *Emergency Librarian, 24*(4), 8–9.

Smith, D. D. (1979). "The Improvement of Children's Oral Reading Through the Use of Teacher Modeling." *Journal of Learning Disabilities*, *12*, 39–42.

Snow, C., Barnes, W., Chandler, J., Goodman, I. F., & Hemphill, L. (1991). *Unfulfilled Expectations: Home and School Influences on Literacy.* Cambridge, MA: Harvard University Press.

———, Burns, M. S., and Griffin, P. (1998). *Preventing Reading Difficulties in Young Children: A Report of the National Research Council.* Washington, DC: National Academy Press.

Stahl, S. A., Duffy-Hester, A., & Stahl, K. A. D. (1998). "Everything You Wanted to Know about Phonics (But Were Afraid to Ask)." *Reading Research Quarterly*, *33*(3), 338—355.

———, Heubach, K., & Cramond, B. (1997). *Fluency-Oriented Reading Instruction.* Athens, GA: National Reading Research Center, University of Georgia.

Stallings, J. (1980). "Allocated Academic Learning Time Revisited, or Beyond Time on Task. *Educational Researcher*, *9*(11), 11–16.

Stayter, F., & Allington, R. L. (1991). "Fluency and Comprehension." *Theory into Practice*.

Stenner, A. J. (1996). *Measuring Reading Comprehension with the Lexile Framework.* Durham, NC: Metametrics.

Stoll, D. R. (1997). *Magazines for Kids and Teens (rev. ed.),* Newark, DE: International Reading Association.

Strickland, D. S., & Walmsley, S. A. (1993). *School Book Clubs and Literacy Development: A Descriptive Study.* M. R. Robinson Foundation.

Swanson, H. L., & Hoskyn, M. (1998). "Experimental Intervention Research on Students with Learning Disabilities: A Meta-Analysis of Treatment Outcomes. *Review of Educational Research*, *68*(3), 277–321.

Taylor, B. M., Frye, B. J., Short, R., & Shearer, B. (1992). "Classroom Teachers Prevent Reading Failure Among Low-Achieving First-Grader Students." *Reading Teacher*, *45*, 592–597.

———, Frye, B. J., & Maruyama, G. M. (1990). "Time Spent Reading and Reading Growth." *American Educational Research Journal*, *27* (#2 Summer), 351–362.

———, Pearson, D., Clark, K., & Walpole, S. (2000). *Beating the odds in teaching all children to read* (Report #2-006). East Lansing, MI: Center for Improving Early Reading Achievement.

Taylor, D. (1998). *Beginning to Read and the Spin Doctors of Science: The Political Campaign to Change America's Mind about How Children Learn to Read.* Urbana, IL: National Council of Teachers of English.

Tharp, R. G., & Gallimore, R. (1989). "Rousing Schools to Life." *American Educator*, *13*(2), 20–25, 46–52.

Thurlow, M., Gaden, J., Ysseldyke, J., & Algozzine, R. (1984). "Student Reading During Reading Class: The Lost Activity in Reading Instruction." *Journal of Educational Research*, *77*(5), 267–272.

Topping, K. (1987). "Peer Tutored Paired Reading: Outcome Data from Ten Projects." *Educational Psychology*, *7*, 604–614.

———, & Ehly, S. (1998). *Peer Assisted Learning.* Mahwah, NJ: Lawrence Erlbaum.

Torgesen, J., & Hecht, S. A. (1996). "Preventing and Remediating Reading Disabilities." In M. Graves, P. van den Brock, & B. Taylor (eds.), *The First R: Every Child's Right to Read*. New York: Teachers College Press (pp. 133–159).

Troia, G. A. (1999). "Phonological Awareness Intervention Research: A Critical Review of the Experimental Methodology." *Reading Research Quarterly*, *34*, 28–53.

Turner, J. C. (1995). "The Influence of Classroom Contexts on Young Children's Motivation for Literacy." *Reading Research quarterly*, *30*(3), 410–441.

Venezky, R. L. (1998). "An Alternate Perspective on Success For All. In K. K. Wong (ed.), *Advances in Educational Policy* (vol. 4, pp. 145–165). Greenwich, CT: JAI Press.

Walmsley, S. A. (1981). "On the Purpose and Content of Secondary Reading Programs: An Educational Ideological Perspective." *Curriculum Inquiry*, *11*(1), 73–93.

Waples, D. (1937/1972). *Social Aspects of Reading in the Depression*. New York, NY: Arno Press.

Wasik, B. A. (1998). "Volunteer Tutoring Programs in Reading: A Review." *Reading Research Quarterly*, *33*(3), 266–293.

———, & Slavin, R. E. (1993). "Preventing Early Reading Failure with One-to-One Tutoring: A Review of Five Programs." *Reading Research Quarterly*, *28*(2), 178–200.

Weber, R. M. (1970). "A Linguistic Analysis of First Grade Reading Errors." *Reading Research Quarterly*, *5*, 427–451.

Wigfield, A. (1997). "Children's Motivations for Reading and Reading Engagement." In J. T. Guthrie & A. Wigfield (eds.), *Reading Engagement: Motivating Readers Through Integrated Instruction* (pp. 14–33). Newark, DE: International Reading Association.

Wilhelm, J. D. (1997). *"You Gotta Be the Book": Teaching Engaged and Reflective Reading with Adolescents*. New York: Teachers College Press.

Wilkinson, I., Wardrop, J., & Anderson, R. C. (1988). "Silent Reading Reconsidered: Reinterpreting Reading Instruction and Its Effects. *American Educational Research Journal*, *25*(1), 127–144.

Worth, J., & McCool, L. S. (1996). "Students Who Say They Hate to Read: The Importance of Opportunity, Choice, and Access." In D. Leu, C. Kinzer, & K. Hinchman (eds.), *Literacies for the 21st Century*. Chicago: National Reading Conference (pp. 245–256).

Ysseldyke, J. E., Thurlow, M. L., Mecklenberg, C., & Graden, J. (1984). "Opportunity to Learn for Regular and Special Education Students During Reading Instruction." *Remedial and Special Education*, *5*, 29–37.

Zigmond, N., Vallecorsa, A., & Leinhardt, J. (1980). "Reading Instruction for Students with Learning Disabilities." *Topics in Language Disorders*, *1*, 89–98.

INDEX